PUBLISHER COMMENTARY

The Risk Management Framework (RMF) is the unified information security framework for the entire federal government that is replacing the legacy Certification and Accreditation (C&A) processes within federal government departments and agencies, the Department of Defense (DOD) and the Intelligence Community (IC). RMF is an integral part of the implementation of FISMA, the Federal Information Security Management Act, and is based on publications of the National Institute of Standards and Technology (NIST) and the Committee on National Security Systems (CNSS). This DoD Instruction provides much needed procedural guidance for the reciprocal acceptance of authorization decisions and artifacts within DoD, and between DoD and other federal agencies, for the authorization and connection of information systems (ISs).

DoD's computer networks have always been targeted for cyber-attacks and now that includes the building controls systems (BCS). Defending a BCS is not as simple at protecting an IT network because most BCS consist of analog equipment that is decades old and retrofit to accept commands from modern digital controllers. Many BCS installations are a hodgepodge of technologies that should have been replaced years ago. DoD is well ahead of industry in this area because DoD recognizes it's a problem whereas most companies are blissfully unaware of their vulnerabilities.

Each of the books we publish includes a list of cybersecurity publications produced by the National Institute of Standards and Technology (NIST), Unified Facilities Criteria (UFC), Mil Handbooks and other publications that are directly applicable to the topic for consideration during the planning process. These publications cover a wide range of cybersecurity concepts that are carefully designed to work together to produce a holistic approach to cybersecurity primarily for government agencies and constitute the best practices used by industry. This holistic strategy to cybersecurity covers the gamut of security subjects from development of secure encryption standards for communication and storage of information while at rest to how best to recover from a cyber-attack.

Why buy a book you can download for free?

Some documents are only distributed in electronic media. Some online docs are missing some pages or the graphics are barely legible. When a new standard is released, an engineer prints it out, punches holes and puts it in a 3-ring binder. While this is not a big deal for a 5 or 10-page document, many cyber documents are over 100 pages and printing a large document is a time-consuming effort. So, an engineer that's paid $75 an hour is spending hours simply printing out the tools needed to do the job. That's time that could be better spent doing engineering. We publish these documents so engineers can focus on what they were hired to do – engineering.

A list of **Cybersecurity Standards** is attached at the end of this document.

Department of Defense
INSTRUCTION

NUMBER 8510.01
March 12, 2014
Incorporating Change 2, July 28, 2017

DoD CIO

SUBJECT: Risk Management Framework (RMF) for DoD Information Technology (IT)

References: See Enclosure 1

1. PURPOSE. This instruction:

a. Reissues and renames DoD Instruction (DoDI) 8510.01 (Reference (a)) in accordance with the authority in DoD Directive (DoDD) 5144.02 (Reference (b)).

b. Implements References (c) through (f) by establishing the RMF for DoD IT (referred to in this instruction as "the RMF"), establishing associated cybersecurity policy, and assigning responsibilities for executing and maintaining the RMF. The RMF replaces the DoD Information Assurance Certification and Accreditation Process (DIACAP) and manages the life-cycle cybersecurity risk to DoD IT in accordance with References (g) through (k).

c. Redesignates the DIACAP Technical Advisory Group (TAG) as the RMF TAG.

d. Directs visibility of authorization documentation and reuse of artifacts between and among DoD Components deploying and receiving DoD IT.

e. Provides procedural guidance for the reciprocal acceptance of authorization decisions and artifacts within DoD, and between DoD and other federal agencies, for the authorization and connection of information systems (ISs).

2. APPLICABILITY

a. This instruction applies to:

(1) OSD, the Military Departments, the Office of the Chairman of the Joint Chiefs of Staff (CJCS) and the Joint Staff, the Combatant Commands, the Office of the Inspector General of the Department of Defense (OIG DoD), the Defense Agencies, the DoD Field Activities, and

all other organizational entities within the Department of Defense (referred to collectively in this instruction as the "DoD Components").

(2) The United States Coast Guard. The United States Coast Guard will adhere to DoD cybersecurity requirements, standards, and policies in this instruction in accordance with the direction in Paragraphs 4a, b, c, and d of the Memorandum of Agreement Between the Department of Defense and the Department of Homeland Security (Reference (q)).

~~(2)~~*(3)* All DoD IT that receive, process, store, display, or transmit DoD information. These technologies are broadly grouped as DoD IS, platform IT (PIT), IT services, and IT products. This includes IT supporting research, development, test and evaluation (T&E), and DoD-controlled IT operated by a contractor or other entity on behalf of the DoD.

b. Nothing in this instruction alters or supersedes the existing authorities and policies of the Director of National Intelligence regarding the protection of sensitive compartmented information (SCI), as directed by Executive Order 12333 (Reference (l)) and other laws and regulations. The application of the provisions and procedures of this instruction to information technologies processing SCI is encouraged where they may complement or cover areas not otherwise specifically addressed.

3. POLICY. It is DoD policy that:

a. The DoD will establish and use an integrated enterprise-wide decision structure for cybersecurity risk management (the RMF) that includes and integrates DoD mission areas (MAs) pursuant to DoDD 8115.01 (Reference (m)) and the governance process prescribed in this instruction.

b. The cybersecurity requirements for DoD information technologies will be managed through the RMF consistent with the principals established in National Institute of Standards and Technology (NIST) Special Publication (SP) 800-37 (Reference (c)). DoD IS and PIT systems will transition to the RMF in accordance with Table 2 of Enclosure 8 of this instruction.

c. The RMF must satisfy the requirements of subchapter III of chapter 35 of Title 44, United States Code (U.S.C.), also known and referred to in this instruction as the "Federal Information Security Management Act (FISMA) of 2002" (Reference (d)). DoD must meet or exceed the standards required by the Office of Management and Budget (OMB) and the Secretary of Commerce, pursuant to FISMA and section 11331 of Title 40, U.S.C. (Reference (n)).

d. All DoD IS and PIT systems must be categorized in accordance with Committee on National Security Systems Instruction (CNSSI) 1253 (Reference (e)), implement a corresponding set of security controls from NIST SP 800-53 (Reference (f)), and use assessment procedures from NIST SP 800-53A (Reference (g)) and DoD-specific assignment values, overlays, implementation guidance, and assessment procedures found on the Knowledge Service (KS) at https://rmfks.osd.mil. As supporting reference security control documents are updated, DoD's implementation of these updates will be coordinated through the RMF TAG.

e. Resources for implementing the RMF must be identified and allocated as part of the Defense planning, programming, budgeting, and execution process.

f. Each DoD IS, DoD partnered system, and PIT system must have an authorizing official (AO) responsible for authorizing the system's operation based on achieving and maintaining an acceptable risk posture.

g. Reciprocal acceptance of DoD and other federal agency and department IS and PIT system authorizations will be implemented to the maximum extent possible. Refusals must be timely, documented, and reported to the responsible DoD Component senior information security officer (SISO) (formerly known as the senior information assurance (IA) officer).

h. All DoD IT identified in paragraph 2a(2) must be under the governance of a DoD Component cybersecurity program in accordance with DoDI 8500.01(Reference (h)).

i. A plan of action and milestones (POA&M) must be developed and maintained to address known vulnerabilities in the IS or PIT system.

j. Continuous monitoring capabilities will be implemented to the greatest extent possible.

k. The RMF process will inform acquisition processes for all DoD IT, including requirements development, procurement, and both developmental T&E (DT&E) and operational T&E (OT&E), but does not replace these processes.

4. RESPONSIBILITIES. See Enclosure 2.

5. PROCEDURES. See Enclosure 3.

6. RELEASABILITY. **Cleared for public release**. This instruction is available on ~~the Internet from the DoD Issuances Website at http://www.dtic.mil/whs/directives.~~ *the Directives Division Website at http://www.esd.whs.mil/DD/.*

7. EFFECTIVE DATE. This instruction is effective March 12, 2014.

Teresa M. Takai
DoD Chief Information Officer

Enclosures
1. References
2. Responsibilities
3. RMF Procedures
4. RMF Governance
5. Cybersecurity Reciprocity
6. Risk Management of IS and PIT Systems
7. KS
8. RMF Transition

Glossary

TABLE OF CONTENTS

TABLES

FIGURES

ENCLOSURE 1

REFERENCES

(a) DoD Instruction 8510.01, "DoD Information Assurance Certification and Accreditation Process (DIACAP)," November 28, 2007 (hereby cancelled)
(b) DoD Directive 5144.02, "DoD Chief Information Officer (DoD CIO)," November 21, 2014
(c) National Institute of Standards and Technology Special Publication 800-37, "Guide for Applying the Risk Management Framework to Federal Information Systems: A Security Life Cycle Approach," February 2010, as amended
(d) Subchapter ~~III~~ *II* of chapter 35 of Title 44, United States Code (also known as the "Federal Information Security ~~Management~~ *Modernization* Act (FISMA) of ~~2002~~ *2014*")
(e) Committee on National Security Systems Instruction 1253, "Security Categorization and Control Selection for National Security Systems," ~~March 15, 2012~~ *March 27, 2014*, as amended
(f) National Institute of Standards and Technology Special Publication 800-53, "Security and Privacy Controls for Federal Information Systems and Organizations," current edition
(g) National Institute of Standards and Technology Special Publication 800-53A, "Guide for Assessing the Security Controls in Federal Information Systems and Organizations: Building Effective Security Assessment Plans," June 2010, as amended
(h) DoD Instruction 8500.01, "Cybersecurity," March 14, 2014
(i) National Institute of Standards and Technology Special Publication 800-39, "Managing Information Security Risk: Organization, Mission, and Information System View," March 2011
(j) National Institute of Standards and Technology Special Publication 800-30, "Guide for Conducting Risk Assessments," September 2012, as amended
(k) DoD Directive 8000.01, "Management of the Department of Defense Information Enterprise (DoD IE)," March 17, 2016
(l) Executive Order 12333, "United States Intelligence Activities," December 4, 1981, as amended
(m) DoD Directive 8115.01, "Information Technology Portfolio Management," October 10, 2005
(n) Section 11331 of Title 40, United States Code
(o) DoD Directive 8140.01, "Cyberspace Workforce Management," August 11, 2015
(p) DoD Instruction 8581.01, "Information Assurance (IA) Policy for Space Systems Used by the Department of Defense," June 8, 2010
(q) DoD Instruction 8320.07, "Implementing the Sharing of Data, Information, and Information Technology (IT) Services in the Department Of Defense," August 3, 2015
(r) DoD Instruction 5000.02, "Operation of the Defense Acquisition System," January 27, 2015*, as amended*
(s) DoD Chief Information Officer Memorandum, "DoD Enterprise Services Designation – Collaboration, Content Discovery, and Content Delivery," February 2, 2009
(t) DoD Chief Information Officer and Intelligence Community Chief Information Officer Memorandum, "Use of Unified Cross Domain Management Office (UCDMO) Baseline Cross Domain Solutions (CDSs)," December 1, 2011

(u) Chairman of the Joint Chiefs of Staff Instruction 6211.02D, "Defense Information Systems Network (DISN) Responsibilities," January 24, 2012
(v) DoD Instruction 8100.04, "DoD Unified Capabilities (UC)," December 9, 2010
(w) DoD Directive 5105.53, "Director of Administration and Management (DA&M)," February 26, 2008
(x) DoD *Manual* 5200.*02*~~-R~~, "*Procedures for the DoD* Personnel Security Program," ~~January 1, 1987, as amended~~ *April 3, 2017*
(y) Public Law 104-191, "Health Insurance Portability and Accountability Act of 1996," August 21, 1996
(z) DoD 8570.01-M, "Information Assurance Workforce Improvement Program," December 19, 2005, as amended
(aa) Appendix III to Office of Management and Budget Circular No. A-130, "Security of Federal Automated Information Resources," November 28, 2000
(ab) Committee on National Security Systems Instruction 4009, "~~National Information Assurance (IA)~~*Committee on National Security Systems (CNSS)* Glossary," ~~April 26, 2010~~ *April 6, 2015*
(ac) National Security Presidential Directive-54, "Cyber Security and Monitoring" /Homeland Security Presidential Directive-23, "Cybersecurity Policy," January 8, 2008[1]
(ad) Memorandum of Agreement Between the Department of Defense and the Department of Homeland Security Regarding Department of Defense and U.S. Coast Guard Cooperation on Cybersecurity and Cyberspace Operations, January 19, 2017[2]

---

[1] Document is classified TOP SECRET. To obtain a copy, fax a request to the Homeland Security Council Executive Secretary at 202-456-5158 and the National Security Council's Senior Director for Records and Access Management at 202-456-9200.

[2] *Available at https://dcms.uscg.afpims.mil/Our-Organization/Assistant-Commandant-for-C4IT-CG-6-/The-Office-of-Information-Management-CG-61/Interagency-Agreements/*

ENCLOSURE 2

RESPONSIBILITIES

1. DoD CHIEF INFORMATION OFFICER (DoD CIO). The DoD CIO:

a. Oversees implementation of this instruction, directs and oversees the cybersecurity risk management of DoD IT, distributes RMF information standards and sharing requirements, and manages the transition from the DIACAP to the RMF.

b. In coordination with the Deputy Assistant Secretary of Defense for Developmental Test and Evaluation (DASD(DT&E)) and the Director, Operational Test and Evaluation (DOT&E), ensures developmental and OT&E activities and findings are integrated into the RMF.

2. DIRECTOR, DEFENSE INFORMATION SYSTEMS AGENCY (DISA). Under the authority, direction, and control of the DoD CIO *and in addition to the responsibilities in paragraph 7 of this enclosure*, the Director, DISA:

a. Ensures control correlation identifiers (CCIs), security requirements guides (SRGs), and security technical implementation guides (STIGs) developed by DISA are consistent with security controls and assessment procedures used by the DoD.

b. Develops and provides RMF training and awareness products and a distributive training capability to support the DoD Components in accordance with Reference (h) and DoDD 8140.01 (Reference (o)); posts the training materials on the IA Support Environment Website (http://iase.disa.mil).

c. Identifies or develops and provides DoD Enterprise RMF management tools.

3. UNDER SECRETARY OF DEFENSE FOR ACQUISITION, TECHNOLOGY, AND LOGISTICS (USD(AT&L)). The USD(AT&L) coordinates with the DoD CIO to ensure RMFs processes are appropriately integrated with Defense Acquisition System processes for acquisitions of DoD IT.

4. DASD(DT&E). Under the authority, direction, and control of the USD(AT&L), the DASD(DT&E), in coordination with the DoD CIO, ensures integration of DT&E activities into the RMF and provides the RMF TAG with input as appropriate or required.

5. DOT&E. The DOT&E:

a. Reviews plans, execution, and results of operational testing to ensure adequate evaluation of cybersecurity for all DoD IT acquisitions subject to oversight.

b. In coordination with DoD CIO, ensures integration of OT&E activities into the RMF and provides the RMF TAG with input as appropriate or required.

6. DIRECTOR, NATIONAL SECURITY AGENCY/CHIEF, CENTRAL SECURITY SERVICE (DIRNSA/CHCSS)). Under the authority, direction, and control of the Under Secretary of Defense for Intelligence *and in addition to the responsibilities in paragraph 7 of this enclosure*, the DIRNSA/CHCSS:

a. Ensures IS security engineering services, when provided to the DoD Components, support the RMF.

b. Develops risk model and risk assessment tools to support authorization decisions.

7. DoD COMPONENT HEADS. The DoD Components heads:

a. Ensure DoD IS and PIT systems are categorized according to the guidelines provided in this instruction.

b. Verify that a program manager (PM) or system manager (SM) is appointed for all ISs and PIT systems.

c. Ensure a trained and qualified AO is appointed in writing for all DoD IS and PIT systems operating within or on behalf of the DoD Component in accordance with Reference (h) and that the systems are authorized in accordance with this instruction.

(1) This role must be assigned to government personnel only. This role may not be re-delegated to personnel that do not also meet these requirements.

(2) Relevant PIT expertise must be a factor in the selection and appointment of AOs responsible for authorizing PIT systems.

d. Develop and issue guidance for PIT systems that reflects DoD Component-unique operational and environmental demands as needed.

e Ensure DoD information technologies under their authority comply with the RMF.

f. Operate only authorized ISs and PIT systems (i.e., those with a current authorization to operate (ATO) or interim authorization to test (IATT)).

g. Comply with all authorization decisions, including denial of authorization to operate (DATO), and enforce authorization termination dates (ATD).

h. Ensure personnel engaged in or supporting the RMF are appropriately trained and possess professional certifications consistent with Reference (o) and supporting issuances.

i. Ensure IS owners (ISOs) appoint user representatives (URs) for DoD IS and PIT systems under the DoD Component's purview.

j. Oversee the DoD Component chief information officer (CIO)'s implementation of this instruction.

k. Ensure participation in the RMF TAG.

l. Ensure that contracts and other agreements include specific requirements in accordance with this instruction.

8. CJCS. In coordination with the DoD CIO *and in addition to the responsibilities in paragraph 7 of this enclosure*, the CJCS ensures the Joint Capabilities Integration and Development System (JCIDS) process supports and documents IS and PIT system categorization consistent with this instruction.

9. COMMANDER, U.S. STRATEGIC COMMAND (USSTRATCOM). *In addition to the responsibilities in paragraph 7 of this enclosure* The Commander, USSTRATCOM:

a. Assigns AOs, issues authorization guidance consistent with this instruction, and resolves authorization issues for space systems used by the DoD in accordance with DoDI 8581.01 (Reference (p)).

b. Serves as the AO for authorizing the processing, storing, or transmitting of nuclear command, control, and communication data on ISs.

ENCLOSURE 3

RMF PROCEDURES

1. OVERVIEW. The forms of DoD IT, as shown in Figure 1, range in size and complexity from individual hardware and software products to stand-alone systems to massive computing environments, enclaves, and networks.

Figure 1. DoD IT

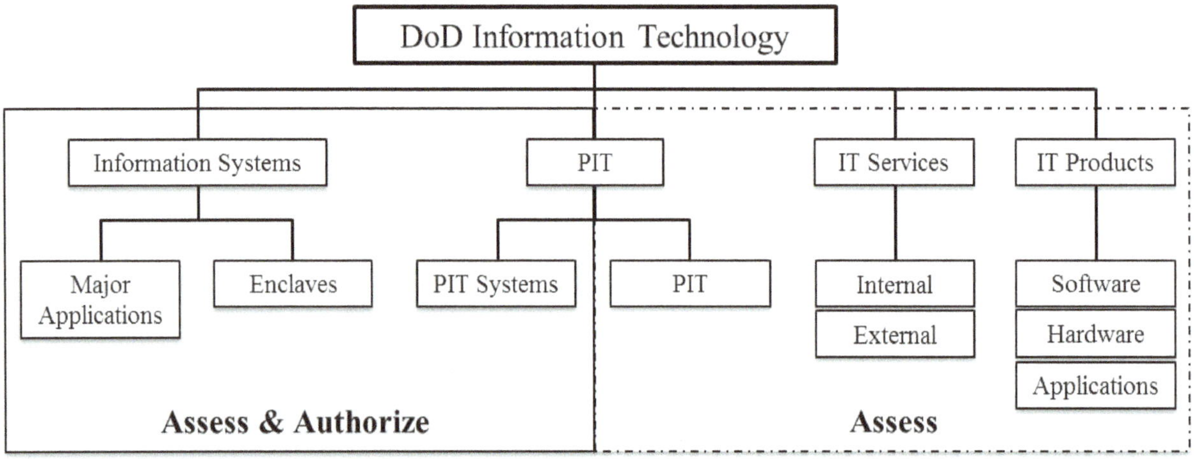

2. RISK MANAGEMENT OF IS AND PIT SYSTEMS. See Enclosure 6.

3. RISK MANAGEMENT OF IT PRODUCTS, SERVICES, AND PIT. IT products, services, and PIT are not authorized for operation through the full RMF process. These types of IT must be securely configured in accordance with applicable DoD policies and security controls and undergo special assessment of their functional and security-related capabilities and deficiencies. The IS security manager (ISSM) (with the review and approval of the responsible AO) is responsible for ensuring all products, services and PIT have completed the appropriate evaluation and configuration processes prior to incorporation into or connection to an IS or PIT system. Paragraphs 3a through 3c summarize the categories of IT, the applicable evaluation process, and associated policy references.

a. IT Products. IT products (including applications), as defined in Reference (h), will be configured in accordance with applicable STIGs under a cognizant ISSM and security control assessor (SCA). STIGs are product-specific and document applicable DoD policies and security requirements, as well as best practices and configuration guidelines. STIGs are associated with security controls through CCIs, which are decompositions of NIST SP 800-53 security controls into single, actionable, measurable items. SRGs are developed by DISA to provide general security compliance guidelines and serve as source guidance documents for STIGs. When a STIG is not available for a product, an SRG may be used. STIGs, SRGs and CCIs are available on the IA Support Environment Website (http://iase.disa.mil). STIG and SRG compliance results for products will be documented as security control assessment results within a product-level security assessment report (SAR) and reviewed by the responsible ISSM (under the direction of the AO) prior to acceptance or connection into an authorized computing environment (e.g., an IS or PIT system with an authorization). This review ensures products will not introduce vulnerabilities into the hosting IS or PIT system. DoD Component-level guidance maximizes testing and review results to minimize duplication of effort across the DoD. See the KS for additional guidance on the review of products.

b. IT Services. IT services are outside the service user organization's authorization boundary, and the service user's organization has no direct control over the application or assessment of required security controls. DoD organizations that use IT services are typically not responsible for authorizing them (i.e., issue an authorization decision).

(1) Internal IT services are delivered by DoD ISs. DoD organizations that use internal IT services must ensure the categorization of the IS delivering the service is appropriate to the needs of the DoD IS using the service, and that written agreements describing the roles and responsibilities of both the providing and the receiving organization are in place.

(2) DoD organizations that use external IT services provided by a non-DoD federal government agency must ensure the categorization of the IS delivering the service is appropriate to the confidentiality, integrity, and availability needs of the information and mission, and that the IS delivering the service is operating under a current authorization from that agency. In accordance with Reference (h), interagency agreements or government statements of work for these external services must contain requirements for service level agreements (SLAs) that include the application of appropriate security controls.

(3) DoD organizations that use external IT services provided by a commercial or other non-federal government entity must ensure the security protections of the IS delivering the service is appropriate to the confidentiality, integrity, and availability needs of the DoD organization's information and mission. DoD organizations must perform categorization in accordance with Reference (e) and tailor appropriately to determine the set of security controls to be included in requests for proposals. DoD organizations will assess the adequacy of security proposed by potential service providers, and accept the proposed approach, negotiate changes to the approach to meet DoD needs, or reject the offer. The accepted security approach must be documented in the resulting contract or order.

(4) DoD organizations contracting for external IT services in the form of commercial cloud computing services must comply with DoD cloud computing policy and procedural guidance as published.

c. PIT. PIT that does not rise to the level of a PIT System may be categorized using Reference (e) with the resultant security control baselines tailored as needed. Otherwise, the specific cybersecurity needs of PIT must be assessed on a case-by-case basis and security controls applied as appropriate.

ENCLOSURE 4

RMF GOVERNANCE

1. RMF GOVERNANCE. The DoD RMF governance structure implements the three-tiered approach to cybersecurity risk management described in NIST SP 800-39 (Reference (i)), synchronizes and integrates RMF activities across all phases of the IT life cycle, and spans logical and organizational entities. These elements are illustrated in Figure 2.

Figure 2. RMF Governance

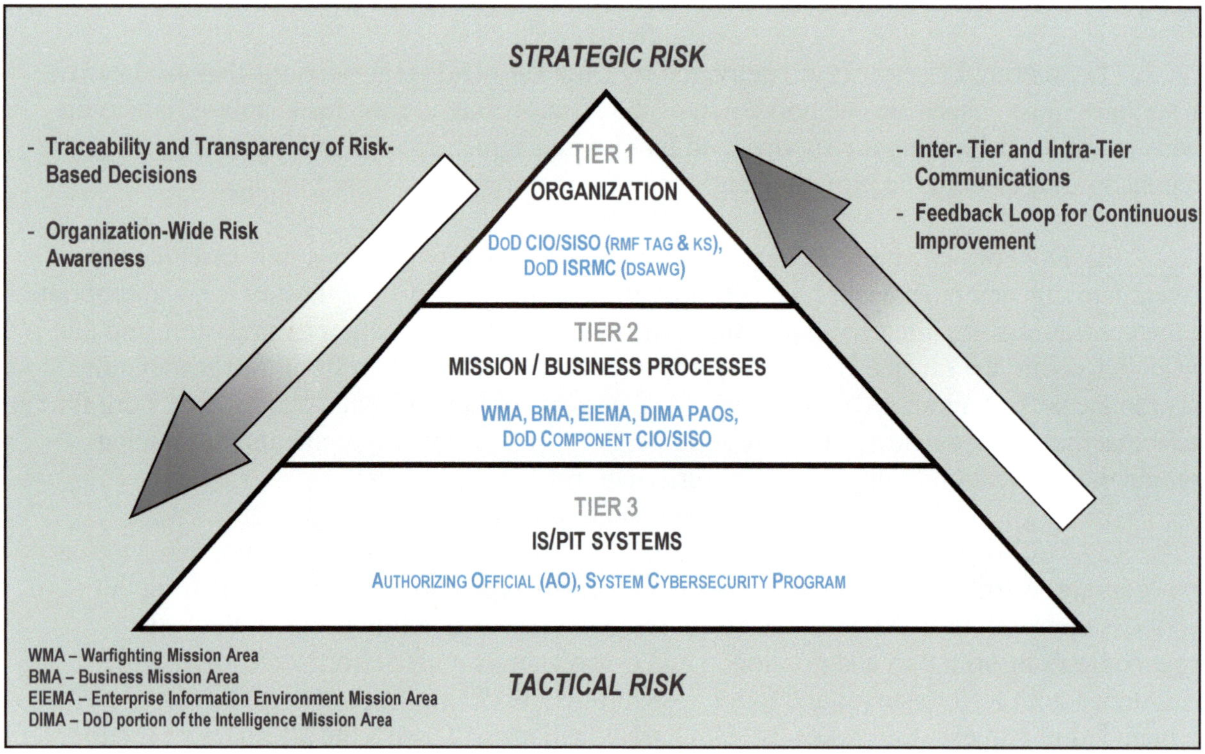

a. Tier 1 – Organization. For the purposes of the RMF, the organization described in Tier 1 is the OSD or strategic level, and it addresses risk management at the DoD enterprise level. The key governance elements in Tier 1 are:

(1) DoD CIO. Directs and oversees the cybersecurity risk management of DoD IT.

(2) Risk Executive Function

(a) DoD Information Security Risk Management Committee (ISRMC) (formerly the Defense Information Systems Network (DISN)/Global Information Grid (GIG) Flag Panel). The DoD ISRMC performs the DoD Risk Executive Function as described in Reference (i). The panel provides strategic guidance to Tiers 2 and 3; assesses Tier 1 risk; authorizes information exchanges and connections for enterprise ISs, cross-MA ISs, cross security domain connections, and mission partner connections.

(b) Defense ~~IA~~ Security*/Cybersecurity* ~~Accreditation~~ *Authorization* Working Group (DSAWG). The DSAWG, in support of the DoD ISRMC, is the community forum for reviewing and resolving authorization issues related to the sharing of community risk. The DSAWG develops and provides guidance to the AOs for IS connections to the DoD Information Enterprise.

(3) DoD SISO. The DoD SISO, in accordance with Reference (h), represents the DoD CIO and directs and coordinates the DoD Cybersecurity Program, which includes the establishment and maintenance of the RMF. In addition, the DoD SISO:

(a) Advises and informs the principal authorizing officials (PAOs) and their representatives.

(b) Oversees the RMF TAG and the online KS.

(4) DoD Cybersecurity Architecture. The DoD Cybersecurity architecture consists of strategies, standards, and plans that have been developed for achieving an assured, integrated, and survivable information enterprise.

(5) The RMF TAG. The RMF TAG (formerly known as the DIACAP TAG) provides implementation guidance for the RMF by interfacing with the DoD Component cybersecurity programs, cybersecurity communities of interest (COIs), and other entities (e.g., DSAWG) to address issues that are common across all entities, by:

(a) Providing detailed analysis and authoring support for the KS.

(b) Recommending changes to security controls in Reference (f), security control baselines and overlays in Reference (e), DoD assignment values, and associated implementation guidance and assessment procedures to the DoD CIO.

(c) Recommending changes to cybersecurity risk management processes to the DoD CIO.

(d) Advising DoD forums established to resolve RMF priorities and cross-cutting issues.

(e) Developing and managing automation requirements for DoD services that support the RMF.

(f) Developing guidance for facilitating RMF reciprocity throughout the DoD.

(6) The KS. The KS, a dynamic online knowledge base, supports RMF implementation, planning, and execution by functioning as the authoritative source for RMF procedures and

guidance. The KS supports RMF practitioners by providing access to DoD security control baselines, security control descriptions, security control overlays, and implementation guidance and assessment procedures, all compliant with References (e) and (f). The KS also supports the RMF TAG by enabling TAG functions and activities, including maintenance of membership; voting, analysis, and authoring; and configuration control of KS enterprise content and functionality. See Enclosure 7 for more information on KS capabilities.

b. Tier 2 - Mission/Business Processes

(1) PAO. A PAO is appointed for each of the DoD MAs (i.e., the warfighting MA (WMA), business MA (BMA), enterprise information environment MA (EIEMA), and DoD portion of the intelligence MA (DIMA)), and their representatives are members of the DoD ISRMC. PAOs must:

(a) Represent the interests of the MA, as defined in Reference (m), and, as required, issues authorization guidance specific to the MA, consistent with this instruction.

(b) Resolve authorization issues within their respective MAs and work with other PAOs to resolve issues among MAs, as needed.

(c) Designate AOs for MA IS and PIT systems supporting MA COIs specified in DoDI 8320.07 (Reference (q)), in coordination with appropriate DoD Component heads, if required.

(d) Designate information security architects or IS security engineers for MA segments or systems of systems, as needed.

(2) DoD Component CIO. Each DoD Component CIO, supported by the DoD Component SISO appointed in accordance with Reference (h), is responsible for administration of the RMF within the DoD Component cybersecurity program; participation in the RMF TAG; visibility and sharing of the RMF status of assigned ISs and PIT systems; and enforcement of training requirements for persons participating in the RMF. DoD Component CIOs must:

(a) Maintain visibility of assessment and authorization status of DoD Component IS and PIT systems through automated assessment and authorization tools or designated repositories for their Component to the DoD CIO and PAOs.

(b) Verify that a PM or SM is identified for each DoD Component IS and PIT system.

(c) Establish and maintain processes and procedures to manage DoD Component POA&Ms.

(d) Appoint a DoD Component SISO to direct and coordinate the DoD Component cybersecurity program.

(e) Review and document concurrence on all ATOs issued for Component IS and PIT systems with a level of risk of "Very High" or "High."

(3) DoD Component SISO. DoD Component SISOs have authority and responsibility for security controls assessment and must establish and manage a coordinated security assessment process for information technologies governed by the DoD Component cybersecurity program. DoD Component SISOs must:

(a) Implement and enforce the RMF within the DoD Component cybersecurity program.

(b) Perform as the SCA or formally delegate the security control assessment role for governed information technologies.

(c) Track the assessment and authorization status of IS and PIT systems governed by the DoD Component cybersecurity program.

(d) Establish and oversee a team of cybersecurity professionals qualified in accordance with Reference (p), responsible for conducting security assessments. DoD Component SISOs may task, organize, staff, and centralize or direct assessment activities to representatives as appropriate. Regardless of the adopted model, the SISO is responsible for assessing quality, capacity, visibility, and effectiveness.

(e) Identify and recommend changes and improvements to the security assessment process, security T&E, and risk assessment methodology, including procedures, risk factors, assessment approach, and analysis approach to the RMF TAG for inclusion in the KS.

(f) Advise AOs on the adequacy of acquisition program implementation of cybersecurity requirements.

(g) Serve as the single cybersecurity coordination point for joint or DoD-wide programs that are deploying information technologies to DoD Component enclaves.

(h) Ensure DoD Component RMF guidance is posted to the DoD Component portion of the KS, and is consistent with DoD policy and guidance.

(i) Oversee DoD Component-level participation in the RMF TAG.

c. Tier 3 – IS and PIT Systems

(1) AO. The DoD Component heads are responsible for the appointment of trained and qualified AOs for all DoD ISs and PIT systems within their Component. AOs should be appointed from senior leadership positions within business owner and mission owner organizations (as opposed to limiting appointments to CIO organizations) to promote accountability in authorization decisions that balance mission and business needs and security concerns. In addition to the responsibilities established in Reference (h), AOs must:

(a) Comply with DoD ISRMC direction issued on behalf of the MA PAOs.

(b) Ensure all appropriate RMF tasks are initiated and completed, with appropriate documentation, for assigned ISs and PIT systems.

(c) Monitor and track overall execution of system-level POA&Ms.

(d) Promote reciprocity to the maximum extent possible.

(e) Not delegate authorization decisions. Other AO responsibilities and tasks may be delegated to formally appointed and qualified AO designated representatives (AODRs).

(2) IS or PIT System Cybersecurity Program. The system cybersecurity program consists of the policies, procedures, and activities of the ISO, PM/SM, UR, ISSM, and IS security officers (ISSOs) at the system level. The system cybersecurity program implements and executes policy and guidance from Tier 1 and Tier 2, and augments them as needed. The system cybersecurity program is responsible for establishing and maintaining the security of the system, including the monitoring and reporting of the system security status. Specific cybersecurity program responsibilities include:

(a) ISOs must:

1. In coordination with the information owner (IO), categorize systems in accordance with Reference (e) and document the categorization in the appropriate JCIDS capabilities document (e.g., capabilities development document).

2. Appoint a UR for assigned IS and PIT systems.

3. Develop, maintain, and track the security plan for assigned IS and PIT systems. (Common security controls owner performs this function for inherited controls.)

(b) PMs (or SM, if no PM is assigned) must:

1. Appoint an ISSM for each assigned IS or PIT system with the support, authority, and resources to satisfy the responsibilities established in this instruction.

2. Ensure each program acquiring an IS or PIT system has an assigned IS security engineer and that they are fully integrated into the systems engineering process.

3. Implement the RMF for assigned IS and PIT systems.

4. Ensure the planning and execution of all RMF activities are aligned, integrated with, and supportive of the system acquisition process.

5. Enforce AO authorization decisions for hosted or interconnected IS and PIT systems.

6. Implement and assist the ISO in the maintenance and tracking of the security plan for assigned IS and PIT systems.

7. Ensure POA&M development, tracking, and resolution.

8. Ensure periodic reviews, testing and assessment of assigned IS and PIT systems are conducted at least annually.

9. Provide the IS or PIT system description.

10. Register the IS or PIT system in the DoD Component registry.

11. Ensure T&E of assigned IS and IT system is planned, resourced, and documented in the program T&E master plan in accordance with DoDI 5000.02 (Reference (r)).

(c) URs must represent the operational and functional requirements of the user community in the RMF process.

(d) ISSMs, in addition to the responsibilities established in Reference (h), must:

1. Support implementation of the RMF.

2. Maintain and report IS and PIT systems assessment and authorization status and issues in accordance with DoD Component guidance.

3. Provide direction to the ISSO in accordance with Reference (h).

4. Coordinate with the organization's security manager to ensure issues affecting the organization's overall security are addressed appropriately.

2. RMF ROLE APPOINTMENT. Table 1 identifies the appropriate authority for the appointment of RMF roles.

Table 1. Appointment of RMF Roles

Role	Appointed By
PAO (formerly principal accrediting authority)	DoD MA owner
DoD SISO (formerly the Senior IA Officer)	DoD CIO
DoD Component CIO	DoD Component head
AO (formerly designated approving (or accrediting) authority)	DoD Component head; PAO for MA-managed ISs
AODR (formerly designated approving (or accrediting) authority representative)	AO
DoD Component SISO	DoD Component CIO or, in organizations in which the position of DoD Component CIO does not exist, the DoD Component head.
SCA (formerly certifying authority)	DoD Component SISO is the Component SCA, but may formally delegate the SCA role as appropriate.
PM/SM	DoD Component head
ISSM (formerly IA manager)	PM or SM
UR	ISO
RMF TAG Representative (formerly DIACAP TAG Representative)	DoD Component SISO

ENCLOSURE 5

CYBERSECURITY RECIPROCITY

1. Cybersecurity reciprocity (referred to in this instruction as "reciprocity") is an essential element in ensuring IT capabilities are developed and fielded rapidly and efficiently across the DoD Information Enterprise. Applied appropriately, reciprocity reduces redundant testing, assessing and documentation, and the associated costs in time and resources. The DoD RMF presumes acceptance of existing test and assessment results and authorization documentation. In order to facilitate reciprocity, the concepts in paragraphs 1a through 1e are fundamental to a common understanding and must be adhered to:

a. IS and PIT systems have only a single valid authorization. Multiple authorizations indicate multiple systems under separate ownership and configuration control.

b. Deploying systems with valid authorizations (from a DoD organization or other federal agency) are intended to be accepted into receiving organizations without adversely affecting the authorizations of either the deployed system or the receiving enclave or site. Deploying system ISOs and PMs must coordinate system security requirement with receiving organizations or their representatives early and throughout system development.

c. An authorization decision for IS or PIT system cannot be made without completing the required assessments and analysis, as recorded in the security authorization package. Deploying organizations must provide the complete security authorization package to receiving organizations. PMs/ ISOs deploying systems across DoD Components will post security authorization documentation to Enterprise Mission Assurance Support Service (eMASS) or other electronic means to provide visibility of authorization status and documentation to planned receiving sites.

d. The process for receiving organization to accept IS and PIT systems is:

(1) Review the complete security authorization package.

(2) Determine the security impact of connecting the deploying system within the receiving enclave or site.

(3) Determine the risk of hosting the deploying system within the enclave or site.

(4) If the risk is acceptable, execute a documented agreement between deploying and receiving organizations (e.g., memorandum of understanding (MOU), memorandum of agreement (MOA), SLA) for the maintenance and monitoring of the security posture of the system (security controls, ~~computer network defense~~ *cybersecurity* service provider (~~CNDSP~~ *CSSP*), etc.).

(5) Document the acceptance by the receiving AO.

(6) Update the receiving enclave or site authorization documentation for inclusion of the deployed system.

e. Receiving organizations have the right to refuse deploying systems due to a security authorization package that does not meet sufficiency and completeness requirements as defined on the KS, or excessive risk to the enclave or site, as determined by the enclave or site AO. Refusals must be documented by the refusing AO, and provided to the deploying organization's ISO or PM, AO, and Component SISO, and to the refusing organization's Component SISO. Disputes should be resolved at the lowest possible level. Disputes that cannot be resolved will be raised to the next appropriate level (e.g., DoD Component, MA PAO, DSAWG, DoD ISRMC).

2. The cases in paragraph 2a through 2e describe the proper application of DoD policy on reciprocity in the most frequently occurring scenarios:

a. A system is authorized by a DoD AO for subsequent deployment into receiving environments authorized by other DoD AOs. This case includes systems designated as enterprise systems in accordance with DoD CIO Memorandum (Reference (s)), as well as non-enterprise systems that will be developed, authorized, and deployed within a single DoD Component, or across multiple DoD Components. Systems with existing authorizations issued by DoD AOs do not require a new authorization to be issued by the receiving enclave or site.

(1) The receiving site executes the acceptance process in paragraph 1d of this enclosure. Issues identified during the acceptance process will be negotiated between the deploying ISO or PM and the receiving enclave or site ISO or SM. Following resolution of any issues, which may result in modifications in either the deploying system or the receiving environment, the deploying system is allowed to be incorporated or connected to the hosting environment. The nature or magnitude of any modifications to the deploying system or receiving site may result in additional assessment activities, but the deploying system and receiving environment retain their own separate authorizations. It is the joint responsibility of the ISOs of deploying systems and the receiving sites to ensure the system design reflects the security, technical and threat environment of the planned receiving sites, as well as leveraging any common controls. Unresolved issues, disputes, and refusals are addressed in accordance with paragraph 1e of this enclosure. Document the acceptance by the receiving AO.

(2) The DoD ISRMC, supported by the DSAWG, may make an enterprise level risk acceptance determination for authorized enterprise systems, which will satisfy the requirements of the first three elements of paragraph 1d of this enclosure. If the DoD ISRMC accepts the risk on behalf of the DoD Information Enterprise, the receiving organization may not refuse to deploy the system.

b. A system is authorized by another U.S. Government agency, and a DoD organization takes ownership of the system for deployment into DoD ISs or enclaves. Systems with an existing authorization issued by other federal agencies require authorization by a DoD AO in accordance with Enclosure 3 of this instruction prior to operating if the providing organization relinquishes configuration and maintenance of the system to the DoD. The receiving enclave or site will maximize reuse of the external agency's security authorization package to support the authorization by the DoD AO. Following the issuance of a DoD authorization, subsequent deployment of the system by the DoD ISO or PM to DoD receiving sites will follow the review and acceptance process described in paragraph 1d of this enclosure.

c. A system is authorized by a DoD organization for its own use, and subsequently provided to another DoD organization for it to use as a separately owned, managed and maintained system. In this case, the receiving organization becomes the ISO and must authorize the system in accordance with Enclosure 3 of this instruction. The receiving enclave or site will maximize reuse of the existing authorization documentation to support the authorization by the receiving AO. Following the issuance of the authorization, subsequent deployment of the system by the system owner to other receiving sites will follow the review and acceptance process described in paragraph 1d of this enclosure.

d. A DoD system is authorized and subsequently deployed for acceptance into receiving sites authorized by a U.S. Government agency other than DoD. In this case, the DoD system's security authorization documentation is made available to the receiving U.S. Government agency. If the receiving agency determines there is insufficient information in the documentation or inadequate security measures in place for establishing an acceptable level of risk, the receiving agency may negotiate with the deploying DoD organization for additional security measures or security-related information. The additional security measures or security-related information may be provided by the DoD organization, the system developer, the receiving agency, some other external third party, or some combination of the above.

e. A DoD organization plans to use an IT service under contract from a commercial entity that has been authorized by a DoD or other U.S. Government agency (e.g., a commercial cloud service authorized by the Federal Risk and Authorization Management Program Joint Authorization Board). In this case, the DoD organization leverages an existing authorization, and maximizes reuse of the existing authorization documentation to support a new authorization by a DoD AO. If the DoD organization determines there are inadequate security measures in place for establishing an acceptable level of risk, the DoD organization may negotiate with IT service provider for additional security measures or security-related information. Upon assessment and approval of all newly included security measures and the documentation of all applicable security measures in the contract agreement with the IT service provider, the DoD organization AO issues an authorization.

ENCLOSURE 6

RISK MANAGEMENT OF IS AND PIT SYSTEMS

1. OVERVIEW. This enclosure describes the DoD process for identifying, implementing, assessing, and managing cybersecurity capabilities and services, expressed as security controls, and authorizing the operation of IS and PIT systems. This enclosure is designed to be a companion guide to Reference (c), providing specific guidance for implementation within DoD. DoD personnel serving in RMF roles at every level should refer to Reference (c) for a full description of the process, definitions, roles and responsibilities, and activities. In cases where Reference (c) conflicts with this instruction, compliance with this instruction takes precedence and is required. The KS also provides expanded coverage of this subject, as well as tools, templates, and best practice information.

a. Applicability. This process is applicable to all IS and PIT systems, as well as DoD partnered systems where it has been agreed that DoD standards will be followed. IT below the system level (e.g., products, IT services) will not be subjected to the full process described in this enclosure. However, IT below the system level must be securely configured (in accordance with applicable DoD policies and security controls), documented in the authorization package and reviewed by the responsible ISSM (under the direction of the AO) for acceptance or connection into an authorized computing environment (i.e., an authorized IS or PIT system).

b. Considerations for Special System Configurations

(1) IS and PIT Systems Implementing a cross domain solution (CDS). CDSs are typically deployed within the IS or PIT system authorization boundary on the system with the higher classification of the cross domain connection, and are included in the IS or PIT system authorization. The AO responsible for the IS or PIT system must consider the security impact of the CDS operation in the overall authorization decision. In addition to the high-side security requirements and ATO, the security requirements for the integrity of the information transfer must be considered and implemented on the connecting low-side IS(s). Additional detail and authoritative guidance is provided in DoD CIO and Intelligence Community CIO Memorandum (Reference (t)) and CJCS Instruction 6211.02D (Reference (u)).

(2) ISs and PIT Systems Providing Unified Capabilities (UC). DoDI 8100.04 (Reference (v)) contains DoD policy for UC, and describes the process for the ~~IA~~ *cybersecurity* certification of UC products. UC products are implemented inside the authorization boundaries of DoD ISs, and the UC product ~~IA~~ *cybersecurity* certification documentation is used to support the overall system assessment and authorization.

(3) Type Authorization. The type authorization is used to deploy identical copies of an IS or PIT system in specified environments. This method allows a single security authorization package to be developed for an archetype (common) version of a system. The system can then be deployed to multiple locations with a set of installation, security control and configuration requirements, or operational security needs that will be provided by the hosting enclave.

(4) Stand-Alone IS and PIT System. Stand-alone IS and PIT systems are types of enclaves that are not interconnected to any other network. Stand-alone IS and PIT systems do not transmit, receive, route, or exchange information outside of the system's authorization boundary. They may range in size from a single workstation to multiple interconnected subsystems as long as they meet the foregoing criteria. Stand-alone IS and PIT systems are authorized as any other IS and PIT systems, but assigned security control sets may be tailored as appropriate with the approval of the AO (e.g., network-related controls may be eliminated). Stand-alone IS and PIT systems must always be clearly identified as such in the authorization documentation. Additionally, identical stand-alone IS and PIT systems that have identical security control implementation and are to be deployed to multiple locations may be type authorized.

(5) DoD-Controlled IS and PIT Systems Operated by a Contractor or Other Entity on Behalf of the DoD. Externally owned IS and PIT systems that are dedicated to DoD processing and are effectively under DoD configuration control must be authorized as DoD IS and PIT systems. A DoD AO must render an authorization decision for this type of a DoD system prior to DoD use of the capability. The following additional requirements apply:

(a) Security responsibilities of the service provider down to the control level must be made explicit in the contract or other binding agreement, along with any other performance and service-level parameters by which the DoD entity will measure the cybersecurity performance of the system for the purpose of authorization.

(b) Technical security of the outsourced environment must be the responsibility of the service provider.

(c) Responsibility for procedural and administrative security will be shared between the service provider and the supported DoD entity contracting for the service.

(d) Security requirements for such a system must be determined by the categorization and control selection process described in paragraphs 2a and 2b of this enclosure, just as for other DoD ISs. Any required security controls that are not explicit in the contract or otherwise covered by a SLA must be assessed as non-compliant (NC). All such NC security controls must be documented in a POA&M with an explanation as to why accepting the risk of operating the system with that control in an NC status is acceptable.

(6) DoD Partnered Systems. DoD partnered systems are ISs or PIT systems that are developed jointly by DoD and non-DoD mission partners, comprise DoD and non-DoD ISs, or contain a mix of DoD and non-DoD information consumers and producers, (e.g., jointly developed systems, multi-national or coalition environments, or first responder environments). Security control selection, system authorization, and other risk management considerations for DoD partnered systems must be clearly defined via a formal partnership agreement, e.g., an MOA, MOU, or SLA. To the extent possible, the negotiated risk management approach should be aligned with the RMF. Regardless of the risk management approach employed, a DoD AO

must render an authorization decision for a DoD partnered system prior to DoD use of the capability.

(7) OSD Systems. Pursuant to DoDD 5105.53 (Reference (w)), the Director of Administration, Office of the Deputy Chief Management Officer of the Department of Defense, is responsible for the IT, including IS and PIT systems, supporting the OSD staff in the National Capital Region.

c. Authorization Approaches. Reference (c) describes three different approaches when planning for and conducting security authorizations. DoD Components may employ any of the following approaches for the authorization of IS and PIT systems:

(1) Authorization with a Single AO. This is the traditional authorization process defined in this enclosure, where a single official in a senior leadership position is both responsible and accountable for a system. The official also accepts the system-related security risks that may impact organizational operations and assets, individuals, other organizations, or the Nation.

(2) Authorization with Multiple AOs. This approach, also known as a joint authorization, is employed when multiple officials either from the same or different organizations, have a shared interest in authorizing a system.

(a) The AOs collectively are responsible and accountable for the system and jointly accept the system-related security risks that may adversely impact organizational operations and assets, individuals, other organizations, and the Nation.

(b) A similar authorization process is followed as with an authorization by a single AO, with the essential difference being the addition of multiple AOs.

(c) Organizations choosing a joint authorization approach are expected to work together on the planning and the execution of RMF tasks, and to formally document their agreement and progress in implementing the tasks. Collaborating on the security categorization, selection of security controls, plan for assessing the controls to determine effectiveness, POA&Ms, and system-level continuous monitoring strategy, is necessary for a successful joint authorization.

(d) The specific terms and conditions of the joint authorization are established by the participating parties in the joint authorization, including for example, the process for ongoing determination and acceptance of risk.

(e) The joint authorization remains in effect only as long as there is mutual agreement among AOs and the authorization meets the requirements established by federal or organizational policies.

(3) Leveraging of an Existing Authorization. The final approach, leveraged authorization, is employed when a DoD AO chooses to accept some or all of the information in an existing security authorization package generated by another federal agency or other DoD

Component (referred to in this instruction as the "owning organization") based on a need to use the same information resources (e.g., IS or services provided by the system). The DoD Component AO reviews the owning organization's security authorization package as the basis for determining risk to the leveraging organization before accepting the authorization. It is DoD policy that the reciprocal acceptance of existing DoD and other federal agency and department system authorizations (i.e., leveraged authorizations), and the artifacts contributing to the authorization decisions, must be employed to the maximum extent. See Enclosure 5 of this instruction and the KS for additional procedural guidance regarding reciprocity.

d. Security Plan. DoD IS and PIT systems must have a security plan that provides an overview of the security requirements for the system and describes the security controls in place or planned for meeting those requirements. The security plan should include implementation status, responsible entities, resources, and estimated completion dates. Security plans may also include, but are not limited to, a compiled list of system characteristics or qualities required for system registration, key security-related documents such as a risk assessment, privacy impact assessment, system interconnection agreements, contingency plan, security configurations, configuration management plan, and incident response plan.

2. RMF STEPS. The RMF consists of the steps depicted in Figure 3. This process parallels the system life cycle, with the RMF activities being initiated at program or system inception (e.g., documented during capabilities identification or at the implementation of a major system modification). However, failure to initiate the RMF at system or program inception is not a justification for ignoring or not complying with the RMF. IS and PIT systems without ATOs must initiate the RMF in accordance with Enclosure 8 of this instruction and Tables 3 and 4, as appropriate, regardless of the system life-cycle stage (e.g., acquisition, operation). Chapter 3 of Reference (c) details the steps of the RMF, and paragraphs 2a through 2f provide amplifying DoD implementation guidance for those steps.

Figure 3. RMF for IS and PIT Systems

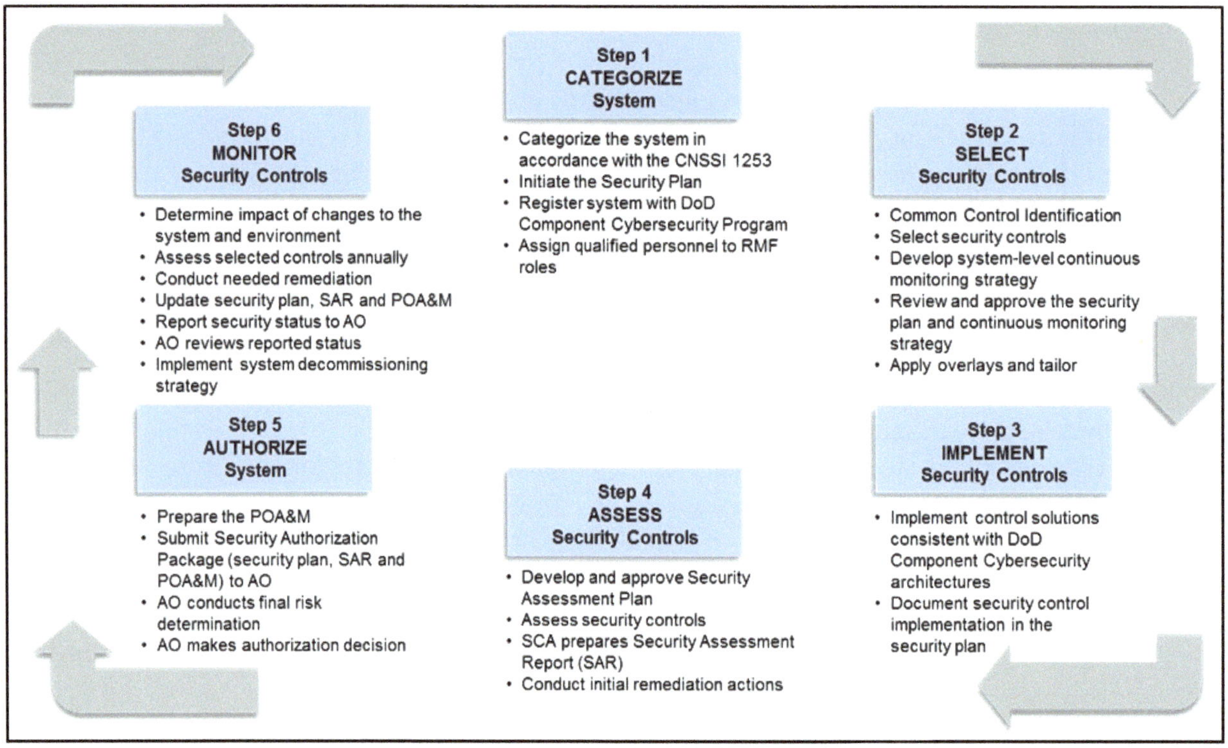

Step 1
CATEGORIZE
System
• Categorize the system in accordance with the CNSSI 1253
• Initiate the Security Plan
• Register system with DoD Component Cybersecurity Program
• Assign qualified personnel to RMF roles
Step 2
SELECT
Security Controls
• Common Control Identification
• Select security controls
• Develop system-level continuous monitoring strategy
• Review and approve the security plan and continuous monitoring strategy
• Apply overlays and tailor
Step 3
IMPLEMENT
Security Controls
• Implement control solutions consistent with DoD Component Cybersecurity architectures
• Document security control implementation in the security plan
Step 4
ASSESS
Security Controls
• Develop and approve Security Assessment Plan
• Assess security controls
• SCA prepares Security Assessment Report (SAR)
• Conduct initial remediation actions
Step 5
AUTHORIZE
System
• Prepare the POA&M
• Submit Security Authorization Package (security plan, SAR and POA&M) to AO
• AO conducts final risk determination
• AO makes authorization decision
Step 6
MONITOR
Security Controls
• Determine impact of changes to the system and environment
• Assess selected controls annually
• Conduct needed remediation
• Update security plan, SAR and POA&M
• Report security status to AO
• AO reviews reported status
• Implement system decommissioning strategy

a. Step 1 - Categorize System

(1) Categorize the system in accordance with Reference (e) and document the results in the security plan. Categorization of IS and PIT systems is a coordinated effort between the PM/SM, ISO, IO, mission owner(s), ISSM, AO, or their designated representatives. In the categorization process, the IO identifies the potential impact (low, moderate, or high) resulting from loss of confidentiality, integrity, and availability if a security breach occurs. For acquisition programs, this categorization will be documented as a required capability in the initial capabilities document, the capability development document, the capabilities production document, and the cybersecurity strategy within the program protection plan (PPP). Specific guidance on determining the security category for information types and ISs is included in the KS.

(2) Describe the system (including system boundary) and document the description in the security plan.

(3) Register the system with the DoD Component Cybersecurity Program. See DoD Component implementing policy for detailed procedures for system registration.

(4) Assign qualified personnel to RMF roles. The members of the RMF Team are required to meet the suitability and fitness requirements established in DoD *Manual* 5200.*02* ~~-R~~ (Reference (x)). RMF Team members must also meet appropriate qualification standards in

accordance with Reference (o). RMF team member assignments must be documented in the security plan.

(5) To avoid potential conflicts of interest or undue influence in RMF roles, certain designations or relationships will not be allowed. The AO or SCA cannot be or report to the PM/SM or program executive officer. The UR cannot be or report to the PM/SM.

b. Step 2 - Select Security Controls

(1) Common Control Identification. This task is the responsibility of the DoD CIO, DoD Component CIOs, and other organizations and entities that provide solutions for common controls. Common controls are selected as "common" and provided via the KS based on risk assessments conducted by these entities at the Tier 1 and Tier 2 levels. By identifying the security controls that are provided by the organization as common solutions for IS and PIT systems, and documenting the assessment and authorization of the controls in a security plan (or equivalent document), individual systems within those organizations can leverage these common controls through inheritance. See the KS for identification of common controls for DoD and additional information on how they are documented within the security authorization package.

(2) Security Control Baseline and Overlay Selection. Identify the security control baseline for the system, as provided in Reference (e), and document in the security plan. The baselines identified in Reference (e) address the overall threat environment for DoD IS and PIT systems. In this step, the applicable security controls baseline and relevant overlays for a system are assigned. See Reference (e) and the KS for detailed procedures. In brief, the process consists of:

(a) Selecting the applicable initial security control baseline from Reference (e) based on the IS categorization. These security control baselines identify the specific security controls from Reference (f) that are applicable to the system categorization.

(b) Identifying overlays that apply to the IS or PIT system due to information contained within the system or environment of operation. Overlays may add or subtract security controls, or provide additional guidance regarding security controls, resulting in a set of security controls applicable to that system that is a combination of the baseline and overlay. The combination of baselines and overlays address the unique security protection needs associated with specific types of information or operational requirements. Overlays reduce the need for ad hoc or case-by-case tailoring by allowing COIs to develop standardized overlays that address their specific needs and scenarios. Access to the overlays, and guidance regarding how to determine which overlays may apply, are included in the KS. The KS is the authoritative source for detailed security control descriptions, implementation guidance and assessment procedures. Examples of overlays include:

1. Tactical environments.

2. PIT systems (including special categories of PIT systems, such as Industrial Control Systems or tactical PIT systems).

3. Personally identifiable information (PII) and Public Law 104-191, also known as the "Health Insurance Portability and Accountability Act" (Reference (y)), requirements.

4. Cross-domain requirements.

5. Classified information.

(c) If necessary, tailor (modify) a control set in response to increased risk from changes in threats or vulnerabilities, or variations in risk tolerance. The resultant set of security controls derived from tailoring is referred to as the tailored control set. Tailoring decisions must be aligned with operational considerations and the environment of the IS or PIT system and should be coordinated with mission owner(s) and URs. Security controls should be added or removed only as a function of specified, risk-based determinations. Tailoring decisions, including the specific rationale (e.g., mapping to risk tolerance) for those decisions, are documented in the security plan for the system. Every selected control must be accounted for either by the organization or the ISO or PM/SM. If a selected control is not implemented, then the rationale for not implementing the controls must be documented in the security plan and POA&M. The tailoring process may include:

1. Applying scoping guidance to the initial set of security controls;

2. Selecting or specifying compensating controls to adjust the initial set of security controls to obtain an equivalent set deemed to be more feasible to implement; or

3. Specifying organization-defined parameters in the security controls via explicit assignment and selection statements to complete the definition of the tailored set of security controls.

(d) Supplementing the tailored baseline security control set, if necessary, with additional controls or control enhancements that consider local conditions including environment of operation, organization-specific security requirements, specific threat information, cost-benefit analyses, or special circumstances, and are based on risk assessments consistent with NIST SP 800-30 (Reference (j)).

(e) The resulting set of security controls is documented, along with the supporting rationale for selection decisions and any system use restrictions, in the security plan. The security plan must identify all common controls inherited from external providers, and establish minimum assurance requirements for those controls.

(3) Monitoring Strategy. Develop and document a system-level strategy for the continuous monitoring of the effectiveness of security controls employed within or inherited by the system, and monitoring of any proposed or actual changes to the system and its environment of operation. The strategy must include the plan for annual assessments of a

subset of implemented security controls, and the level of independence required of the assessor (e.g., ISSM or SCA). The breadth, depth, and rigor of these annual assessments should be reflective of the security categorization of the system and threats to the system. The SCA should be integral to the development of this strategy. The system-level continuous monitoring strategy must conform to all applicable published DoD enterprise-level or DoD Component-level continuous monitoring strategies.

(4) Security Plan and System-Level Continuous Monitoring Strategy Review and Approval. The DoD Components will develop and implement processes whereby the AO (or designee) reviews and approves the security plan and system-level continuous monitoring strategy submitted by the ISO or PM/SM. By approving the security plan, the AO agrees to the system categorization, the set of security controls proposed to meet the security requirements for the system, and the adequacy of the system-level continuous monitoring strategy. The approval of the security plan also establishes the level of effort required to successfully complete the remainder of the steps in the RMF and provides the basis of the security specification for the acquisition of the system, subsystems, or components. For acquisition programs, approval should be accomplished before Milestone B and the issuance of the design and development request for proposals. If the security plan is deemed unacceptable, the AO or designated representative sends the plan back to the ISO or PM/SM for appropriate action. The AO approval of the security plan must be documented in the security plan.

c. Step 3 - Implement Security Controls

(1) Implement the security controls specified in the security plan in accordance with DoD implementation guidance found on the KS.

(a) Products used within an IS or PIT system boundary will be configured in accordance with applicable STIGs or SRGs where STIGs are not available.

(b) Security controls are implemented consistent with DoD and DoD Component ~~IA~~ *cybersecurity* architectures and standards, employing system and software engineering methodologies, security engineering principles, and secure coding techniques. DoD recommended security control implementation guidance is available on the KS.

(c) The ISO or PM/SM must ensure early and ongoing involvement by IS security engineers qualified in accordance with DoD 8570.01-M (Reference (z)). Mission owner(s) must translate security controls into system specifications, ensure the successful integration of those specifications into the system design, and ensure security engineering trades do not impact the ability of the system to meet the fundamental mission requirements. This includes ensuring that technical and performance requirements derived from the assigned security controls are included in requests for proposals and subsequent contract documents for design, development, production, and maintenance.

(d) The proposed system security design must be addressed in preliminary and critical design reviews. System security design should address security controls that may be satisfied through inheritance of common controls. In addition, mandatory configuration settings are established and implemented on IT products in accordance with federal and DoD policies.

(e) PMs for programs acquiring IS or PIT systems in accordance with Reference (r) must integrate the security engineering of cybersecurity requirements and cybersecurity testing considerations into the program's systems engineering, development test and evaluation, and program protection planning processes.

(2) Document the security control implementation in accordance with DoD implementation guidance found on the KS, in the security plan, providing a description of the control implementation (including planned inputs, expected behavior, and expected outputs) if not in accordance with the KS guidance. See the KS for specific control documentation requirements, including required artifacts, templates, and best practices.

(3) Security controls that are available for inheritance (e.g. common controls) by IS and PIT systems will be identified and have associated compliance status provided by hosting or connected systems.

d. Step 4 - Assess Security Controls

(1) Develop, review, and approve a plan to assess the security controls. An assessment methodology consistent with Reference (j) is provided in the KS as a model for use or adaptation. DoD Components will use this model, or justify the use of another risk assessment methodology within the Component, to include addressing understanding of the impact on reciprocity across the federal, Intelligence, and DoD communities. The risk assessment will be used by the SCA to determine the level of overall system cybersecurity risk and as a basis for a recommendation for risk acceptance or denial to the AO. The SCA develops the security assessment plan, and the AO or AODR reviews and approves the plan. PMs of programs acquiring IS and PIT systems, in concert with the SCA and the program's T&E, working-level integrated product team, must:

(a) Ensure security control assessment activities are coordinated with the following: interoperability and supportability certification efforts; DT&E events; OT&E events.

(b) Ensure the coordination of activities is documented in the security assessment plan and the program T&E documentation to maximize effectiveness, reuse, and efficiency. Where appropriate, integrated testing should include the evaluation of survivability, assessment of controls, and certification testing, as well as developmental and OT&E.

(2) Assess the security controls in accordance with the security assessment plan and DoD assessment procedures. Assessment procedures are used to verify that a security control has been properly implemented. SRG and STIG compliance results will be documented and used as part of the overall security control assessment. The KS is the authoritative source for security control assessment procedures. Actual results are recorded in the SAR and POA&M as part of the security authorization package, along with any artifacts produced during the assessment (e.g., output from automated test tools or screen shots that depict aspects of system configuration). For

inherited security controls, assessment test results and supporting documentation are maintained by the providing system and are made available to SCAs of receiving systems on request. For common controls inherited from the enterprise, instructions for documenting compliance are provided on the KS. SCAs will maximize the reuse of existing assessment (i.e., a leveraged authorization), and T&E documentation in their assessment of the system.

(a) Record Security Control Compliance Status. If no vulnerabilities are found through the process of executing the assessment procedures, the security control is recorded as compliant. If vulnerabilities are found, the control is recorded as NC in the POA&M, with sufficient explanation. Security controls that are not technically or procedurally relevant to the system, as determined by the AO, will be recorded as not applicable (NA) in the POA&M, with sufficient justification. The status and results of all security control assessments in the control set (see paragraph 2b(2) of this enclosure) will be recorded in the SAR. DoD implementation guidance and assessment procedures are available on the KS. Assessment procedures that are used that are not in accordance with the KS will be documented fully in the SAR.

(b) Assign Vulnerability Severity Value for Security Controls. Vulnerability severity values are assigned to all NC controls by the SCA as part of the security control analysis to indicate the severity associated with the identified vulnerability. Vulnerability severity values are identified in Reference (j). Vulnerability severity values for security controls are informed by assessment at the CCI level. If a control has a STIG or SRG associated through CCIs, the vulnerabilities identified by STIG or SRG assessments will be used to inform the overall vulnerability severity value for the security control.

(c) Determine Risk Level for Security Controls. The SCA determines and documents in the SAR a risk level for every NC security control in the system baseline. NC controls are subjected to a risk assessment process that considers multiple factors in producing the risk level. As described in Reference (j), these factors include, but are not limited to:

1. The SCA's determination that a credible or validated threat source and potential event exists that is capable of, and likely to, exploit vulnerabilities in the implementation of the control.

2. Vulnerability severity level and pre-disposing conditions. This includes the SCA's estimate of the adequacy of existing mitigations or compensating controls to address the vulnerability and mitigations provided by the hosting enclave, ~~CNDSP~~ *CSSP*, or other protective measures.

3. The cybersecurity attribute (i.e., confidentiality, integrity, or availability) and associated categorization impact level (high, moderate, low) related to the control.

4. The SCA's estimate of impact of a successful threat event.

(d) Assess and Characterize Aggregate Level of Risk to the System. The SCA must determine and document in the SAR an assessment of overall system level of risk (see levels of risk in Reference (j)), and identify the key drivers for the assessment. The SCA's risk assessment considers threats, vulnerabilities, and potential impacts as well as existing and planned risk mitigation. The risk assessment must address all NC controls, and clearly communicate the SCA's conclusion on system cybersecurity risk, and any recommendations for special instructions to accompany the authorization decision.

(3) Prepare the SAR, documenting the issues, findings, and recommendations from the security control assessment. The SAR documents the SCA's findings of compliance with assigned security controls based on actual assessment results. It addresses security controls in a NC status, including existing and planned mitigations. A SAR is always required before an authorization decision. If a compelling mission or business need requires the rapid introduction of a new IS or PIT system, assessment activity and a SAR are still required.

(4) Conduct remediation actions on NC security controls based on the findings and recommendations of the SAR and reassess remediated control(s), as appropriate.

e. Step 5 - Authorize System

(1) Prepare the POA&M based on the vulnerabilities identified during the security control assessment. A full discussion and templates for preparing a POA&M is provided in the KS.

(a) A POA&M that the ISO or PM/SM develops:

1. Identifies tasks that need to be accomplished to remediate or mitigate vulnerabilities.

2. Specifies resources required to accomplish the elements of the plan.

3. Includes milestones for completing tasks and their scheduled completion dates.

(b) POA&Ms are maintained throughout the system life cycle. Once posted to the POA&M, vulnerabilities will be updated after correction or mitigation actions are completed, but not removed.

(c) Inherited vulnerabilities must be addressed on the POA&Ms. POA&Ms must be active throughout a system's life cycle as vulnerabilities remain or are remediated.

(d) The AOs, or AODRs, must monitor and track overall execution of POA&Ms under their responsibility.

(e) The ISO or PM/SM must implement the corrective actions identified in the POA&M. With the support and assistance of the ISSM, they must also provide visibility and status to the AO and the SISO.

(f) The DoD Component SISOs must monitor and track the overall execution of system-level POA&Ms across the entire Component until identified security vulnerabilities have been remediated and the RMF documentation is appropriately adjusted.

(2) Assemble the security authorization package and submit the package to the AO for adjudication. The ISSM assembles the security authorization package, consisting of the updated security plan, the SAR, and the POA&M. The security authorization package must also contain, or provide links to, the appropriate documentation for any security controls that are being satisfied through inheritance (e.g., security authorization packages, contract documents, MOAs, and SLAs). The security authorization package is submitted to the AO (via the AODR if appropriate) for review and final acceptance.

(3) Determine the risk to organizational operations (including mission, functions, image, or reputation), organizational assets, individuals, other organizations, or the Nation. The AO considers the current security state of the system (as reflected by the risk assessment and recommendations provided in the SAR), and weighs this against the operational need for the system. The AO must also consider any applicable risk-related guidance from the DoD SISO, PAOs, DoD ISRMC, DSAWG, DoD Component SISO, or mission owner(s). Weighing these factors, the AO renders a final determination of risk to DoD operations and assets, individuals, other organizations, and the Nation from the operation and use of the system. The KS provides additional guidance and tools for conducting system authorization risk assessments.

(4) Determine if the risk to organizational operations, organizational assets, individuals, other organizations, or the Nation is acceptable. The product of this risk determination is the authorization decision. An authorization decision applies to a specifically identified IS or PIT system and balances mission need against risk to the mission, the information being processed, the broader information environment, and other missions reliant on the shared information environment. A DoD authorization decision is expressed as an ATO, an IATT, or a DATO. An IS or PIT system is considered unauthorized if an authorization decision has not been made.

(a) If overall risk is determined to be acceptable, and there are no NC controls with a level of risk of "Very High" or "High," then the authorization decision should be issued in the form of an ATO. An ATO authorization decision must specify an ATD that is within 3 years of the authorization date unless the IS or PIT system has a system-level continuous monitoring program compliant with DoD continuous monitoring policy as issued.

(b) If NC controls with a level of risk of "Very High" or "High" exist that cannot be corrected or mitigated immediately, but overall system risk is determined to be acceptable due to mission criticality, then the authorization decision will be issued in the form of an ATO with conditions and only with permission of the responsible DoD Component CIO. If the system still requires operation with a level of risk of "Very High" or "High" after 1 year, the DoD Component CIO must again grant permission for continued operation of the system. This authority cannot be delegated below the DoD Component CIO. The DoD Component CIO must concur in writing or through DoD public key infrastructure (PKI)-certified digital signature that the security risk of continued system operation is acceptable due to mission criticality. The DoD Component CIO provides a copy of the concurrence and authorization decision document with supporting rationale to the DoD ISRMC Secretariat and the DoD SISO. This authorization decision closely manages risk while allowing system operation. The ATOs with conditions should specify an AO review period that is within 6 months of the authorization date. The POA&M supporting this ATO documents identified vulnerabilities and specifies corrective actions to be completed before the review.

(c) If the risk determination is being made to permit testing of the system in an operational information environment or with live data, and the risk is acceptable, then the authorization decision should be issued in the form of an IATT.

1. IATTs should be granted only when an operational environment or live data is required to complete specific test objectives (e.g., replicating certain operating conditions in the test environment is impractical), and should expire at the completion of testing (normally for a period of less than 90 days). Operation of a system under an IATT in an operational environment is for testing purposes only (i.e., the system will not be used for operational purposes during the IATT period). The application of an IATT in support of DT&E needs to be planned, resourced, and documented within the program T&E plan in accordance with Reference (r).

2. For full and independent operational testing, an ATO (rather than an IATT) may be required if operational testing and evaluation is being conducted in the operational environment or on deployed capabilities. In this case, the ATO should be reviewed following operational testing and evaluation for modification as necessary in consideration of the operational test results.

3. All applicable security controls should be tested and satisfied before testing in an operational environment or with live data except for those that can only be tested in an operational environment. In consultation with the ISO or PM/SM, the AO will determine which security controls can only be tested in an operational environment.

(d) If risk is determined to be unacceptable, the authorization decision should be issued in the form of a DATO. If the system is already operational, the AO will issue a DATO and stop operation of the system immediately. Network connections will be immediately terminated for any system issued a DATO. A DATO may also be issued coincidental to implementing a decommissioning strategy for a system.

(e) Documentation supporting an authorization decision will be provided in electronic form if requested by AOs of interconnecting IS and PIT systems.

f. Step 6 - Monitor Security Controls

(1) Determine the security impact of proposed or actual changes to the IS or PIT system and its environment of operation. Included in the security controls assigned to all IS and PIT systems are security controls related to configuration and deficiency management, performance monitoring, and periodic independent evaluations (e.g., penetration testing).

(a) The ISSM, in coordination with other appropriate personnel (e.g., IS security engineer, system administrators, ~~CNDSP~~ *CSSP*):

1. Continuously monitors the system or information environment for security-relevant events and configuration changes that negatively affect security posture.

2. Periodically assesses the quality of security controls implementation against performance indicators, such as: security incidents; feedback from external inspection agencies (e.g., OIG DoD, Government Accountability Office (GAO)); exercises; and operational evaluations, including Director, OT&E ~~IA,~~ assessments.

3. Must report any significant change in the security posture of the system, and recommended mitigations, immediately to the SCA and AO.

4. May recommend to the SCA or AO a reassessment of any or all security controls at any time.

(2) Assess a subset of the security controls employed within and inherited by the IS or PIT system in accordance with the AO-approved system-level continuous monitoring strategy.

(a) The assessor must provide a written and signed (or if digital, DoD PKI-certified digitally signed) report in the SAR format to the AO that indicates the results of an annual assessment of selected security controls. Reference (c) provides additional guidance on conducting annual assessments.

(b) The results of the annual assessment must be documented in an SAR, which will recommend either no change to the authorization status or downgrade to a DATO. The POA&M will also be updated as appropriate.

(c) The AO must review the SAR in light of mission and information environment indicators and determine a course of action that will be provided to the responsible CIO or SISO for reporting requirements described in FISMA. An AO may downgrade or revoke an authorization decision at any time if risk conditions or concerns so warrant.

(3) Conduct remediation actions based on the results of ongoing monitoring activities, assessment of risk, and outstanding items in the POA&M. Systems with a current ATO that are found to be operating in an unacceptable cybersecurity posture through Director, OT&E ~~IA,~~ assessments, GAO audits, OIG DoD audits, or other reviews or events (such as an annual security review or compliance assessment) must have the newly identified vulnerabilities and associated level of risk added to an existing or newly created POA&M.

(4) The PM/SM ensures the security plan and POA&M are updated based on the results of the system-level continuous monitoring process. The ISSM may recommend changes or improvement to the implementation of assigned security controls, the assignment of additional security controls, or changes or improvements to the design of the system itself to the SCA and AO at any time.

(5) Report the security status of the system (including the effectiveness of security controls employed within and inherited by the system) to the AO and other appropriate organizational officials on an ongoing basis in accordance with the monitoring strategy.

(6) The AO reviews the reported security status of the system (including the effectiveness of security controls employed within and inherited by the system) on an ongoing basis in accordance with the monitoring strategy to determine whether the risk to organizational operations, organizational assets, individuals, other organizations, or the nation remains acceptable.

(a) In accordance with Appendix III to OMB Circular A-130 (Reference (aa)), systems must be reassessed and reauthorized once every 3 years. The results of an annual review or a major change in the cybersecurity posture at any time may also indicate the need for reassessment and reauthorization of the system.

(b) Systems that have been evaluated as having a sufficiently robust system-level continuous monitoring program (as defined by emerging DoD continuous monitoring policy) may operate under a continuous reauthorization. Continuous monitoring does not replace the security authorization requirement; rather, it is an enabler of ongoing authorization decisions.

(7) Implement a system decommissioning strategy, when needed, which executes required actions when an IS or PIT system is removed from service. When a system is removed from operation, a number of RMF-related actions are required. Before decommissioning, any control inheritance relationships should be reviewed and assessed for impact. Once the system has been decommissioned, the security plan should be updated to reflect the system's decommissioned status, and the system should be removed from all tracking systems. Other artifacts and supporting documentation should be disposed of according to its sensitivity or classification. Data or objects in cybersecurity infrastructures that support the DoD Information Enterprise, such as key management, identity management, vulnerability management, and privilege management, should be reviewed for impact.

3. <u>INTEGRATING THE RMF INTO THE DEFENSE ACQUISITION MANAGEMENT SYSTEM</u>. The RMF is designed to be complementary to and supportive of DoD's acquisition management system activities, milestones, and phases. RMF activities should be initiated as early as possible in the DoD acquisition process to increase security and decrease cost. Requirements development, procurement, and T&E processes should be considered in applying the RMF to the acquisition of DoD IT. Threats to these systems should be designated consistent with the most severe risk to any individual component or subcomponent for consideration of requirements, acquisition, and testing and evaluation. Figure 4 illustrates the alignment of RMF steps to the acquisition life cycle.

Figure 4. RMF and the Defense Acquisition Management System

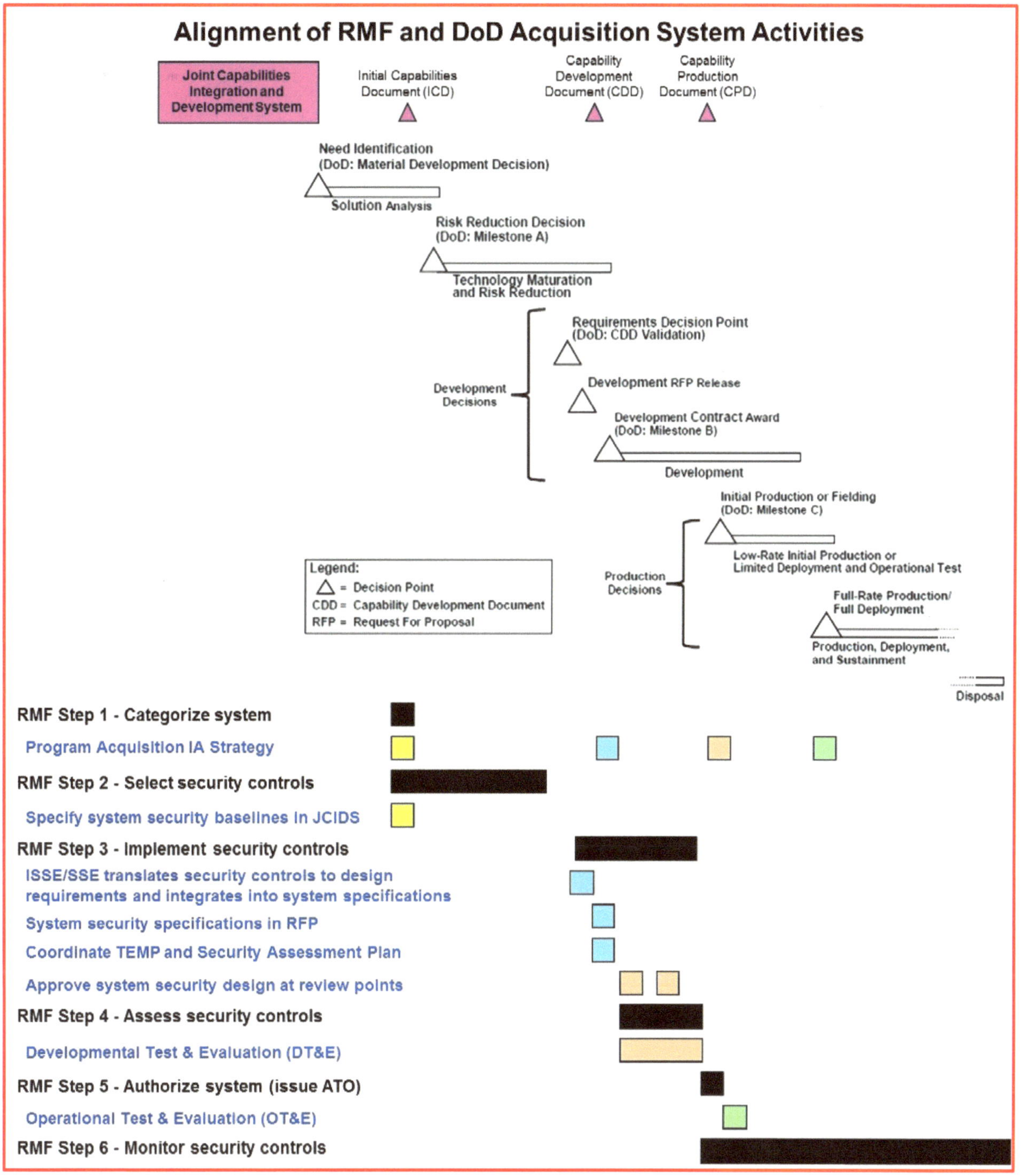

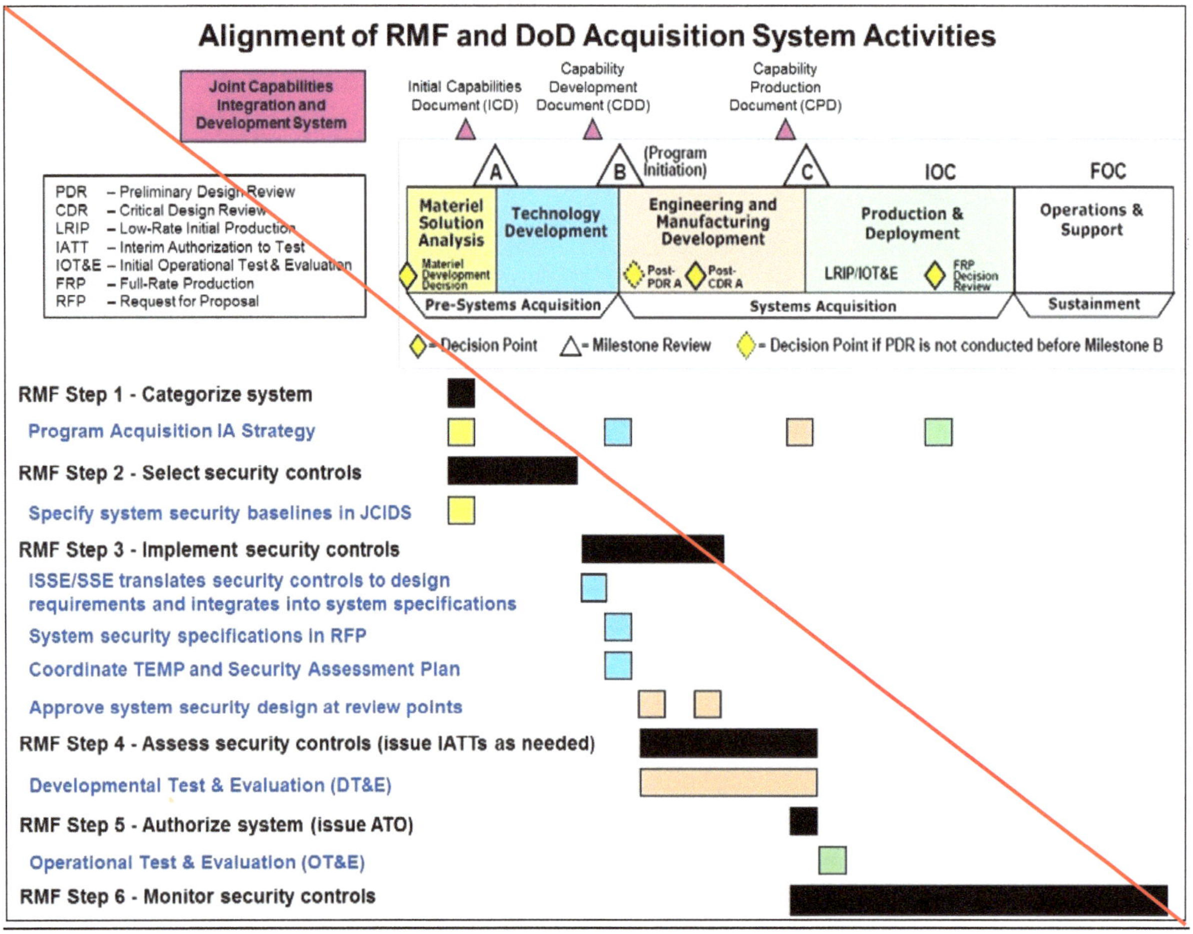

4. <u>SECURITY AUTHORIZATION DOCUMENTATION</u>. The security authorization documentation consists of all artifacts developed through RMF activity. Security authorization documentation is maintained throughout a system's life cycle. The security authorization package consists of the security plan, SAR, POA&M, risk assessment report, authorization decision document, and is the minimum information necessary for the acceptance of an IS or PIT system by a receiving organization. Detailed information on the content of the security authorization package is available on the KS.

ENCLOSURE 7

KS

1. DoD RMF practitioners need ready access to RMF policy and guidance to effectively and efficiently apply the appropriate methods, standards, and practices required to protect DoD IT. Implementation guidance must reflect the most up-to-date DoD intent regarding evolving security objectives and risk conditions. To address this enterprise challenge, the KS was established as the online, web-based resource that:

a. Provides guidance and tools for implementing and executing the RMF.

b. Is the authoritative source for RMF guidance and the repository for DoD RMF policy.

c. Is available to all individuals with IT risk management responsibilities.

d. Provides convenient access to security controls baselines, overlays, individual security controls and security control implementation guidance and assessment procedures.

e. Supports automated and non-automated implementation of the RMF.

2. The KS website (https://rmfks.osd.mil) is accessible by individuals with a DoD PKI certificate (common access card (CAC)), or External Certification Authority certificate in conjunction with DoD sponsorship (e.g., for DoD contractors without a CAC and who work off-site).

3. The KS hosts a library of tools, diagrams, process maps, documents, etc., to support and aid in the execution of the RMF. It is also a collaboration workspace for the RMF user community to develop, share, and post lessons learned, best practices, cybersecurity news and events, and other cybersecurity-related information resources.

4. The RMF TAG is responsible for the functional configuration and content management of the KS, and provides detailed analysis and authoring support for the enterprise portion of the KS content.

ENCLOSURE 8

RMF TRANSITION

1. DoD IS and PIT systems will transition to the RMF in accordance with Table 2. All IS and PIT systems must transition to the Reference (e) categorization and security controls selection methodology, Reference (f) security control catalog, and the RMF.

2. Components are authorized and encouraged to start using RMF immediately. Recognizing the transition to RMF is complex; Table 2 establishes the timeline for the authorized continued use of DIACAP.

3. There are three key events in Table 2:

a. The date the package is submitted to the AO; this date determines the maximum duration of the ATO.

b. The date the package is signed by the AO (i.e. ATO date); this date starts the clock on the ATO.

c. The ATD, based on the maximum duration of the ATO, is calculated from the AO signature date/ATO Date.

4. Table 2 provides a staggered timeline, and ATO duration for IS and PIT systems under the DIACAP. The timelines apply to new system authorizations as well as existing systems with an expiring ATO. All IS and PIT systems must comply.

5. In the case of significant financial or operational impacts of transitioning to RMF, an AO may submit a request for deviation from this guidance for specific systems to the respective DoD Component CIO for approval. All requests for deviation forwarded to the Component CIO must be accompanied by an IS transition plan and a plan of action and milestones.

Table 2. RMF Initial Transition Timeline and Instructions

Completed DIACAP Package Submitted to AO for Signature	ATO Date	Maximum Duration of ATO under DIACAP
Signature date of this document through May 31, 2015	Determined by AO Signature Date	2.5 years from AO signature date
June 1, 2015 through February 1, 2016		2 years from AO signature date
February 2, 2016 through October 1, 2016		1.5 years from AO signature date

6. Transition to updated versions of Reference (e) will be in accordance with Table 3 for IS and PIT systems that have transitioned to the RMF.

Table 3. Transition Timeline and Instructions – Updates to CNSSI 1253

	DoD System Authorization Status	Transition Timeline and Instructions (Upon publication of future versions of CNSSI 1253)
1	New start or unauthorized operational system (No initiated RMF activity or Component PIT system certification and accreditation activity).	Transition to new versions of CNSSI 1253 within 6 months of publication of updates and execute RMF.
2	System has initiated RMF, but has not yet begun executing the security plan.	Transition to new versions of CNSSI 1253 within 6 months of publication of updates and execute RMF.
3	System has begun executing the RMF security plan.	Either: a. Continue under the current version of CNSSI 1253. Develop a strategy and schedule for transitioning to the new version of CNSSI 1253. Obtain AO's approval of the strategy and schedule. The schedule for transitioning must not exceed the system re-authorization timeline. Or; b. Transition to the new version of CNSSI 1253 and execute RMF.
4	System has an RMF or equivalent DoD Component PIT system authorization decision that is current within 3 years.	Develop a strategy and schedule for transitioning to the new version of CNSSI 1253. Obtain AO's approval of the strategy and schedule. The schedule for transitioning must not exceed the system re-authorization timeline.
5	System has an RMF or equivalent DoD Component PIT system authorization that is more than 3 years old.	Transition to the new version of CNSSI 1253 immediately and execute RMF.

GLOSSARY

PART I. ABBREVIATIONS AND ACRONYMS

AO	authorizing official
AODR	authorizing official designated representative
ATD	authorization termination date
ATO	authorization to operate
BMA	business mission area
CAC	common access card
CCI	control correlation identifier
CDS	cross domain solution
CIO	chief information officer
CJCS	Chairman of the Joint Chiefs of Staff
~~CNDSP~~ *CSSP*	~~computer network defense~~ *cybersecurity* service provider
CNSSI	Committee on National Security Systems Instruction
COI	community of interest
DASD(DT&E)	Deputy Assistant Secretary of Defense for Developmental Test and Evaluation
DATO	denial of authorization to operate
DIACAP	DoD Information Assurance Certification and Accreditation Process
DIMA	DoD portion of the intelligence mission area
DIRNSA/CHCSS	Director, National Security Agency/Chief, Central Security Service
DISA	Defense Information Systems Agency
DISN	Defense Information Systems Network
DoD CIO	DoD Chief Information Officer
DoD ISRMC	DoD Information Security Risk Management Committee
DoDD	DoD Directive
DoDI	DoD Instruction
DOT&E	Director, Operational Test and Evaluation
DSAWG	Defense ~~IA~~ Security *Cybersecurity* ~~Accreditation~~ *Authorization* Working Group
DT&E	developmental test and evaluation
EIEMA	enterprise information environment mission area
eMASS	Enterprise Mission Assurance Support Service
FISMA	Federal Information Security Management Act
GAO	Government Accountability Office
~~GIG~~	~~Global Information Grid~~

IA	information assurance
IATT	interim authorization to test
IO	information owner
IS	information system
ISO	information system owner
ISRMC	Information Security Risk Management Committee
ISSM	information system security manager
ISSO	information system security officer
IT	information technology
JCIDS	Joint Capabilities Integration and Development System
KS	Knowledge Service
MA	mission area
MOA	memorandum of agreement
MOU	memorandum of understanding
NA	not applicable
NC	non-compliant
NIST	National Institute of Standards and Technology
OIG DoD	Office of the Inspector General of the Department of Defense
OMB	Office of Management and Budget
OT&E	operational test and evaluation
PAO	principal authorizing official
PII	personally identifiable information
PIT	platform information technology
PKI	public key infrastructure
PM	program manager
PM/SM	program manager/system manager
POA&M	plan of action and milestones
PPP	program protection plan
RMF	risk management framework
SAR	security assessment report
SCA	security control assessor
SCI	sensitive compartmented information
SISO	senior information security officer
SLA	service level agreement
SM	system manager
SP	Special Publication
SRG	security requirements guide
STIG	security technical implementation guide

TAG	Technical Advisory Group
T&E	test and evaluation
UC	unified capabilities
UR	user representative
U.S.C.	United States Code
USD(AT&L)	Under Secretary of Defense for Acquisition, Technology, and Logistics
USSTRATCOM	United States Strategic Command
WMA	warfighting mission area

PART II. DEFINITIONS

Unless otherwise noted, these terms and their definitions are for the purposes of this instruction.

application. Defined in CNSSI 4009 (Reference (ab)).

authorization. Defined in Reference (c).

authorization boundary. Defined in Reference (c).

AO. Defined in Reference (ab).

AODR. An organizational official acting on behalf of an AO in carrying out and coordinating the required activities associated with security authorization

ATO. Defined in Reference (ab).

CCI. Defined in Reference (h).

CDS. Defined in Reference (ab).

common controls. Defined in Reference (c).

cybersecurity. Prevention of damage to, protection of, and restoration of computers, electronic communications systems, electronic communications services, wire communication, and electronic communication, including information contained therein, to ensure its availability, integrity, authentication, confidentiality, and nonrepudiation. Defined in National Security Presidential Directive-54/Homeland Security Presidential Directive-23 (Reference (ac)).

DoD Information Enterprise. Defined in DoDD 8000.01 (Reference (k)).

DoD IT. Defined in Reference (h).

enclave. Defined in Reference (ab).

hardware. Defined in Reference (ab).

IATT. Defined in Reference (ab).

IT product. Defined in Reference (h).

IT Service. Defined in Reference (h).

IO. Defined in Reference (ab).

IS. Defined in Reference (ab).

ISO. Defined in Reference (c), but for the purposes of this instruction is not synonymous with "PM" as indicated in Reference (c).

ISSM. Defined in Reference (ab).

ISSO. Defined in Reference (ab).

MA. Defined in Reference (m).

Milestone B. Defined in Reference (r).

mission partners. Defined in Reference (k).

network. Defined in Reference (ab).

penetration testing. Defined in Reference (ab).

PIT. Defined in Reference (h).

PIT system. Defined in Reference (h).

PM/SM. Defined in Reference (h).

POA&M. Defined in Reference (ab).

reciprocity. Defined in Reference (ab).

risk. Defined in Reference (ab).

risk assessment. Defined in Reference (ab).

risk executive function. Defined in Reference (ab).

risk management. Defined in Reference (ab).

risk mitigation. Defined in Reference (ab).

RMF. Defined in Reference (ab).

SAR. Provides a disciplined and structured approach for documenting the findings of the assessor and the recommendations for correcting any identified vulnerabilities in the security controls.

SCA. Defined in Reference (c).

SCI. Defined in Reference (ab).

security. Defined in Reference (ab).

security assessment plan. Provides the objectives for the security control assessment and a detailed roadmap of how to conduct such an assessment. See Reference (g) for additional information regarding security assessment plans.

security control assessment. Defined in Reference (ab).

security control baseline. Defined in Reference (ab).

security controls. Defined in Reference (ab).

security domain. Defined in Reference (ab).

security plan. Defined in Reference (c).

SLA. Defined in Reference (ab).

software. Defined in Reference (ab).

SRG. Defined in Reference (h).

STIG. Defined in Reference (h).

type authorization. A method of system authorization that allows a single security authorization package to be developed for an archetype (common) version of a system, and the issuance of a single authorization decision that is applicable to multiple deployed instances of the system.

UC. Defined in Reference (v).

UR. Defined in Reference (ab).

CyberSecurity Standards Library™

NIST SP 500-288 Specification for WS-Biometric Devices (WS-BD)
NIST SP 500-291 V2 NIST Cloud Computing Standards Roadmap
NIST SP 500-292 NIST Cloud Computing Reference Architecture
NIST SP 500-293 V1 & V2 US Government Cloud Computing Technology Roadmap
NIST SP 500-293 V3 US Government Cloud Computing Technology Roadmap
NIST SP 500-299 NIST Cloud Computing Security Reference Architecture
NIST SP 500-304 Data Format for the Interchange of Fingerprint, Facial & Other Biometric Information
NIST SP 800-1 Bibliography of Selected Computer Security Publications January 1980-October 1989
NIST SP 800-12 R1 An Introduction to Information Security
NIST SP 800-13 Telecommunications Security Guidelines for Telecommunications Management Network
NIST SP 800-14 Generally Accepted Principles and Practices for Securing Information Technology Systems
NIST SP 800-15 V1 Minimum Interoperability Specification for PKI Components (MISPC)
NIST SP 800-16 R1 A Role-Based Model for Federal Information Technology/Cybersecurity Training
NIST SP 800-17 Modes of Operation Validation System (MOVS): Requirements and Procedures
NIST SP 800-18 R1 Developing Security Plans for Federal Information Systems
NIST SP 800-19 Mobile Agent Security
NIST SP 800-20 Modes of Operation Validation System for the Triple Data Encryption Algorithm
NIST SP 800-22 R1a A Statistical Test Suite for Random and Pseudorandom Number Generators for Cryptographic Applications
NIST SP 800-23 Guidelines to Federal Organizations on Security Assurance and Acquisition/Use of Tested/Evaluated Products
NIST SP 800-24 PBX Vulnerability Analysis - Finding Holes in Your PBX Before Someone Else Does
NIST SP 800-25 Federal Agency Use of Public Key Technology for Digital Signatures and Authentication
NIST SP 800-27 Rev A Engineering Principles for Information Technology Security (A Baseline for Achieving Security)
NIST SP 800-28 Guidelines on Active Content and Mobile Code
NIST SP 800-29 A Comparison of the Security Requirements for Cryptographic Modules in FIPS 140-1 and FIPS 140-2
NIST SP 800-30 Guide for Conducting Risk Assessments
NIST SP 800-31 Intrusion Detection Systems
NIST SP 800-32 Public Key Technology and the Federal PKI Infrastructure
NIST SP 800-33 Underlying Technical Models for Information Technology Security
NIST SP 800-34 R1 Contingency Planning Guide for Federal Information Systems
NIST SP 800-35 Guide to Information Technology Security Services
NIST SP 800-36 Guide to Selecting Information Technology Security Products
NIST SP 800-37 R2 Applying Risk Management Framework to Federal Information
NIST SP 800-38 Recommendation for Block Cipher Modes of Operation
NIST SP 800-38A Addendum Block Cipher Modes of Operation: Three Variants of Ciphertext Stealing for CBC Mode
NIST SP 800-38B Block Cipher Modes of Operation: The CMAC Mode for Authentication
NIST SP 800-38C Block Cipher Modes of Operation: The CCM Mode for Authentication and Confidentiality
NIST SP 800-38D Block Cipher Modes of Operation: Galois/Counter Mode (GCM) and GMAC
NIST SP 800-38E Block Cipher Modes of Operation: The XTS-AES Mode for Confidentiality on Storage Devices
NIST SP 800-38F Block Cipher Modes of Operation: Methods for Key Wrapping
NIST SP 800-38G Block Cipher Modes of Operation: Methods for Format-Preserving Encryption
NIST SP 800-39 Managing Information Security Risk
NIST SP 800-40 R3 Guide to Enterprise Patch Management Technologies
NIST SP 800-41 Guidelines on Firewalls and Firewall Policy
NIST SP 800-43 Systems Administration Guidance for Securing Microsoft Windows 2000 Professional System
NIST SP 800-44 V2 Guidelines on Securing Public Web Servers
NIST SP 800-45 V2 Guidelines on Electronic Mail Security
NIST SP 800-46 R2 Guide to Enterprise Telework, Remote Access, and Bring Your Own Device (BYOD) Security
NIST SP 800-47 Security Guide for Interconnecting Information Technology Systems
NIST SP 800-48 Guide to Securing Legacy IEEE 802.11 Wireless Networks
NIST SP 800-49 Federal S/MIME V3 Client Profile
NIST SP 800-50 Building an Information Technology Security Awareness and Training Program
NIST SP 800-51 R1 Guide to Using Vulnerability Naming Schemes
NIST SP 800-52 R1 Guidelines for the Selection, Configuration, and Use of Transport Layer Security (TLS) Implementations
NIST SP 800-53 R5 Security and Privacy Controls for Information Systems and Organizations
NIST SP 800-53A R4 Assessing Security and Privacy Controls
NIST SP 800-54 Border Gateway Protocol Security
NIST SP 800-55 R1 Performance Measurement Guide for Information Security
NIST SP 800-56A R3 Pair-Wise Key-Establishment Schemes Using Discrete Logarithm Cryptography
NIST SP 56B R 1 Recommendation for Pair-Wise Key-Establishment Schemes Using Integer Factorization Cryptography
NIST SP 800-56C R1 Recommendation for Key-Derivation Methods in Key-Establishment Schemes - Draft
NIST SP 800-57 R4 Recommendation for Key Management
NIST SP 800-58 Security Considerations for Voice Over IP Systems
NIST SP 800-59 Guideline for Identifying an Information System as a National Security System
NIST SP 800-60 Guide for Mapping Types of Information and Information Systems to Security Categories
NIST SP 800-61 R2 Computer Security Incident Handling Guide
NIST SP 800-63-3 Digital Identity Guidelines
NIST SP 800-63a Digital Identity Guidelines - Enrollment and Identity Proofing
NIST SP 800-63b Digital Identity Guidelines - Authentication and Lifecycle Management
NIST SP 800-63c Digital Identity Guidelines- Federation and Assertions
NIST SP 800-64 R2 Security Considerations in the System Development Life Cycle

CyberSecurity Standards Library™

NIST SP 800-65 Integrating IT Security into the Capital Planning and Investment Control Process
NIST SP 800-66 Implementing the Health Insurance Portability and Accountability Act (HIPAA) Security Rule
NIST SP 800-67 R2 Recommendation for Triple Data Encryption Algorithm (TDEA) Block Cipher - Draft
NIST SP 800-68 R1 Guide to Securing Microsoft Windows XP Systems for IT Professionals: A NIST Security Configuration Checklist
NIST SP 800-69 Guidance for Securing Microsoft Windows XP Home Edition: A NIST Security Configuration Checklist
NIST SP 800-70 R4 National Checklist Program for IT Products
NIST SP 800-72 Guidelines on PDA Forensics
NIST SP 800-73-4 Interfaces for Personal Identity Verification
NIST SP 800-76-2 Biometric Specifications for Personal Identity Verification
NIST SP 800-77 Guide to IPsec VPNs
NIST SP 800-78-4 Cryptographic Algorithms and Key Sizes for Personal Identity Verification
NIST SP 800-79-2 Authorization of Personal Identity Verification Card Issuers (PCI) and Derived PIV Credential Issuers (DPCI)
NIST SP 800-81-2 Secure Domain Name System (DNS) Deployment Guide
NIST SP 800-82 R2 Guide to Industrial Control Systems (ICS) Security
NIST SP 800-83 Guide to Malware Incident Prevention and Handling for Desktops and Laptops
NIST SP 800-84 Guide to Test, Training, and Exercise Programs for IT Plans and Capabilities
NIST SP 800-85A-4 PIV Card Application and Middleware Interface Test Guidelines
NIST SP 800-85B-4 PIV Data Model Test Guidelines - Draft
NIST SP 800-86 Guide to Integrating Forensic Techniques into Incident Response
NIST SP 800-87 R1 Codes for Identification of Federal and Federally-Assisted Organizations
NIST SP 800-88 R1 Guidelines for Media Sanitization
NIST SP 800-89 Recommendation for Obtaining Assurances for Digital Signature Applications
NIST SP 800-90A R1 Random Number Generation Using Deterministic Random Bit Generators
NIST SP 800-90B Recommendation for the Entropy Sources Used for Random Bit Generation
NIST SP 800-90C Recommendation for Random Bit Generator (RBG) Constructions - 2nd Draft
NIST SP 800-92 Guide to Computer Security Log Management
NIST SP 800-94 Guide to Intrusion Detection and Prevention Systems (IDPS)
NIST SP 800-95 Guide to Secure Web Services
NIST SP 800-97 Establishing Wireless Robust Security Networks: A Guide to IEEE 802.11i
NIST SP 800-98 Guidelines for Securing Radio Frequency Identification (RFID) Systems
NIST SP 800-100 Information Security Handbook: A Guide for Managers
NIST SP 800-101 R1 Guidelines on Mobile Device Forensics
NIST SP 800-102 Recommendation for Digital Signature Timeliness
NIST SP 800-106 Randomized Hashing for Digital Signatures
NIST SP 800-107 R1 Recommendation for Applications Using Approved Hash Algorithms
NIST SP 800-108 Recommendation for Key Derivation Using Pseudorandom Functions
NIST SP 800-111 Guide to Storage Encryption Technologies for End User Devices
NIST SP 800-113 Guide to SSL VPNs
NIST SP 800-114 R1 User's Guide to Telework and Bring Your Own Device (BYOD) Security
NIST SP 800-115 Technical Guide to Information Security Testing and Assessment
NIST SP 800-116 A Recommendation for the Use of PIV Credentials in PACS - Draft
NIST SP 800-117 V1.2 Guide to Adopting and Using the Security Content Automation Protocol (SCAP) - Draft
NIST SP 800-119 Guidelines for the Secure Deployment of IPv6
NIST SP 800-120 Recommendation for EAP Methods Used in Wireless Network Access Authentication
NIST SP 800-121 R2 Guide to Bluetooth Security
NIST SP 800-122 Guide to Protecting the Confidentiality of Personally Identifiable Information
NIST SP 800-123 Guide to General Server Security
NIST SP 800-124 R1 Managing the Security of Mobile Devices in the Enterprise
NIST SP 800-125 (A & B) Secure Virtual Network Configuration for Virtual Machine (VM) Protection
NIST SP 800-126 R3 Technical Specification for the Security Content Automation Protocol (SCAP)
NIST SP 800-126A SCAP 1.3 Component Specification 3 Version Updates
NIST SP 800-127 Guide to Securing WiMAX Wireless Communications
NIST SP 800-128 Guide for Security-Focused Configuration Management of Information Systems
NIST SP 800-130 A Framework for Designing Cryptographic Key Management Systems
NIST SP 800-131A R1 Transitions: Recommendation for Transitioning the Use of Cryptographic Algorithms and Key Lengths
NIST SP 800-132 Recommendation for Password-Based Key Derivation - Part 1: Storage Applications
NIST SP 800-133 Recommendation for Cryptographic Key Generation
NIST SP 800-135 R1 Recommendation for Existing Application-Specific Key Derivation Functions
NIST SP 800-137 Information Security Continuous Monitoring (ISCM)
NIST SP 800-142 Practical Combinatorial Testing
NIST SP 800-144 Guidelines on Security and Privacy in Public Cloud Computing
NIST SP 800-145 The NIST Definition of Cloud Computing
NIST SP 800-146 Cloud Computing Synopsis and Recommendations
NIST SP 800-147 BIOS Protection Guidelines & BIOS Integrity Measurement Guidelines
NIST SP 800-147B BIOS Protection Guidelines for Servers
NIST SP 800-150 Guide to Cyber Threat Information Sharing
NIST SP 800-152 A Profile for U.S. Federal Cryptographic Key Management Systems
NIST SP 800-153 Guidelines for Securing Wireless Local Area Networks (WLANs)
NIST SP 800-154 Guide to Data-Centric System Threat Modeling

CyberSecurity Standards Library™

NIST SP 800-155 BIOS Integrity Measurement Guidelines
NIST SP 800-156 Representation of PIV Chain-of-Trust for Import and Export
NIST SP 800-157 Guidelines for Derived Personal Identity Verification (PIV) Credentials
NIST SP 800-160 Systems Security Engineering
NIST SP 800-161 Supply Chain Risk Management Practices for Federal Information Systems and Organizations
NIST SP 800-162 Guide to Attribute Based Access Control (ABAC) Definition and Considerations
NIST SP 800-163 Vetting the Security of Mobile Applications
NIST SP 800-164 Guidelines on Hardware- Rooted Security in Mobile Devices Draft
NIST SP 800-166 Derived PIV Application and Data Model Test Guidelines
NIST SP 800-167 Guide to Application Whitelisting
NIST SP 800-168 Approximate Matching: Definition and Terminology
NIST SP 800-171 R1 Protecting Controlled Unclassified Information in Nonfederal Systems
NIST SP 800-175 (A & B) Guideline for Using Cryptographic Standards in the Federal Government
NIST SP 800-177 R1 Trustworthy Email
NIST SP 800-178 Comparison of Attribute Based Access Control (ABAC) Standards for Data Service Applications
NIST SP 800-179 Guide to Securing Apple OS X 10.10 Systems for IT Professional
NIST SP 800-180 NIST Definition of Microservices, Application Containers and System Virtual Machines
NIST SP 800-181 National Initiative for Cybersecurity Education (NICE) Cybersecurity Workforce Framework
NIST SP 800-183 Networks of 'Things'
NIST SP 800-184 Guide for Cybersecurity Event Recovery
NIST SP 800-185 SHA-3 Derived Functions: cSHAKE, KMAC, TupleHash and ParallelHash
NIST SP 800-187 Guide to LTE Security - Draft
NIST SP 800-188 De-Identifying Government Datasets - (2nd Draft)
NIST SP 800-190 Application Container Security Guide
NIST SP 800-191 The NIST Definition of Fog Computing
NIST SP 800-192 Verification and Test Methods for Access Control Policies/Models
NIST SP 800-193 Platform Firmware Resiliency Guidelines
NIST SP 1800-1 Securing Electronic Health Records on Mobile Devices
NIST SP 1800-2 Identity and Access Management for Electric Utilities 1800-2a & 1800-2b
NIST SP 1800-2 Identity and Access Management for Electric Utilities 1800-2c
NIST SP 1800-3 Attribute Based Access Control NIST 1800-3a & 3b
NIST SP 1800-3 Attribute Based Access Control NIST 1800-3c Chapters 1 - 6
NIST SP 1800-3 Attribute Based Access Control NIST1800-3c Chapters 7 - 10
NIST SP 1800-4a & 4b Mobile Device Security: Cloud and Hybrid Builds
NIST SP 1800-4c Mobile Device Security: Cloud and Hybrid Builds
NIST SP 1800-5 IT Asset Management: Financial Services
NIST SP 1800-6 Domain Name Systems-Based Electronic Mail Security
NIST SP 1800-7 Situational Awareness for Electric Utilities
NIST SP 1800-8 Securing Wireless Infusion Pumps
NIST SP 1800-9a & 9b Access Rights Management for the Financial Services Sector
NIST SP 1800-9c Access Rights Management for the Financial Services Sector - How To Guide
NIST SP 1800-11a & 11b Data Integrity Recovering from Ransomware and Other Destructive Events
NIST SP 1800-11c Data Integrity Recovering from Ransomware and Other Destructive Events - How To Guide
NIST SP 1800-12 Derived Personal Identity Verification (PIV) Credentials
NISTIR 7100 PDA Forensic Tools: An Overview and Analysis
NISTIR 7188 Specification for the Extensible Configuration Checklist Description Format (XCCDF)
NISTIR 7200 Proximity Beacons and Mobile Device Authentication: An Overview and Implementation
NISTIR 7206 Smart Cards and Mobile Device Authentication: An Overview and Implementation
NISTIR 7250 Cell Phone Forensic Tools: An Overview and Analysis
NISTIR 7275 V1.1 Specification for the Extensible Configuration Checklist Description Format (XCCDF)
NISTIR 7275 R4 V1.2 Specification for the Extensible Configuration Checklist Description Format (XCCDF)
NISTIR 7284 Personal Identity Verification Card Management Report
NISTIR 7290 Fingerprint Identification and Mobile Handheld Devices: An Overview and Implementation
NISTIR 7298 R2 Glossary of Key Information Security Terms
NISTIR 7316 Assessment of Access Control Systems
NISTIR 7337 Personal Identity Verification Demonstration Summary
NISTIR 7358 Program Review for Information Security Management Assistance (PRISMA)
NISTIR 7359 Information Security Guide for Government Executives
NISTIR 7387 Cell Phone Forensic Tools: An Overview and Analysis Update
NISTIR 7435 The Common Vulnerability Scoring System (CVSS) and Its Applicability to Federal Agency Systems
NISTIR 7452 Secure Biometric Match-on-Card Feasibility Report
NISTIR 7497 Security Architecture Design Process for Health Information Exchanges (HIEs)
NISTIR 7502 The Common Configuration Scoring System (CCSS): Metrics for Software Security Configuration Vulnerabilities
NISTIR 7511 R4 V1.2 Security Content Automation Protocol (SCAP) Version 1.2 Validation Program Test Requirements
NISTIR 7516 Forensic Filtering of Cell Phone Protocols
NISTIR 7539 Symmetric Key Injection onto Smart Cards
NISTIR 7551 A Threat Analysis on UOCAVA Voting Systems
NISTIR 7559 Forensics Web Services (FWS)
NISTIR 7564 Directions in Security Metrics Research
NISTIR 7581 System and Network Security Acronyms and Abbreviations

Click on a title to obtain a printed copy of these standards at Amazon.com

CyberSecurity Standards Library™

NISTIR 7601 Framework for Emergency Response Officials (ERO)
NISTIR 7611 Use of ISO/IEC 24727
NISTIR 7617 Mobile Forensic Reference Materials: A Methodology and Reification
NISTIR 7621 R1 Small Business Information Security: The Fundamentals
NISTIR 7622 Notional Supply Chain Risk Management Practices for Federal Information Systems
NISTIR 7628 R1 Vol 1 Guidelines for Smart Grid Cybersecurity - Architecture, and High-Level Requirements
NISTIR 7628 R1 Vol 2 Guidelines for Smart Grid Cybersecurity - Privacy and the Smart Grid
NISTIR 7628 R1 Vol 3 Guidelines for Smart Grid Cybersecurity - Supportive Analyses and References
NISTIR 7658 Guide to SIMfill Use and Development
NISTIR 7676 Maintaining and Using Key History on Personal Identity Verification (PIV) Cards
NISTIR 7682 Information System Security Best Practices for UOCAVA-Supporting Systems
NISTIR 7692 V2 Specification for the Open Checklist Interactive Language (OCIL)
NISTIR 7693 Specification for Asset Identification 1.1
NISTIR 7694 Specification for the Asset Reporting Format 1.1
NISTIR 7696 V2.3 Common Platform Enumeration: Name Matching Specification
NISTIR 7697 V2.3 Common Platform Enumeration: Dictionary Specification
NISTIR 7698 V2.3 Common Platform Enumeration: Applicability Language Specification
NISTIR 7711 Security Best Practices for the Electronic Transmission of Election Materials for UOCAVA Voters
NISTIR 7756 CAESARS Framework Extension: An Enterprise Continuous Monitoring Technical Refer
NISTIR 7764 Status Report on the Second Round of the SHA-3 Cryptographic Hash Algorithm Competition
NISTIR 7770 Security Considerations for Remote Electronic UOCAVA Voting
NISTIR 7771 V2 Conformance Test Architecture for Biometric Data Interchange Formats - Beta
NISTIR 7773 An Application of Combinatorial Methods to Conformance Testing for Document Object Model Events
NISTIR 7788 Security Risk Analysis of Enterprise Networks Using Probabilistic Attack Graphs
NISTIR 7791 Conformance Test Architecture and Test Suite for ANSI/NIST-ITL 1-2007
NISTIR 7799 Continuous Monitoring Reference Model, Workflow, and Specifications - Draft
NISTIR 7800 Applying the Continuous Monitoring Technical Reference Model to the Asset, Configuration, and Vulnerability Management Domains - Draft
NISTIR 7823 Advanced Metering Infrastructure Smart Meter Upgradeability Test Framework
NISTIR 7874 Guidelines for Access Control System Evaluation Metrics
NISTIR 7904 Trusted Geolocation in the Cloud: Proof of Concept Implementation
NISTIR 7924 Reference Certificate Policy
NISTIR 7987 Policy Machine: Features, Architecture, and Specification
NISTIR 8006 NIST Cloud Computing Forensic Science Challenges
NISTIR 8011 Vol 1 Automation Support for Security Control Assessments
NISTIR 8011 Vol 2 Automation Support for Security Control Assessments
NISTIR 8040 Measuring the Usability and Security of Permuted Passwords on Mobile Platforms
NISTIR 8053 De-Identification of Personal Information
NISTIR 8054 NSTIC Pilots: Catalyzing the Identity Ecosystem
NISTIR 8055 Derived Personal Identity Verification (PIV) Credentials (DPC) Proof of Concept Research
NISTIR 8060 Guidelines for the Creation of Interoperable Software Identification (SWID) Tags
NISTIR 8062 Introduction to Privacy Engineering and Risk Management in Federal Systems
NISTIR 8074 Vol 1 & Vol 2 Strategic U.S. Government Engagement in International Standardization to Achieve U.S. Objectives for Cybersecurity
NISTIR 8080 Usability and Security Considerations for Public Safety Mobile Authentication
NISTIR 8089 An Industrial Control System Cybersecurity Performance Testbed
NISTIR 8112 Attribute Metadata - Draft
NISTIR 8135 Identifying and Categorizing Data Types for Public Safety Mobile Applications
NISTIR 8138 Vulnerability Description Ontology (VDO)
NISTIR 8144 Assessing Threats to Mobile Devices & Infrastructure
NISTIR 8151 Dramatically Reducing Software Vulnerabilities
NISTIR 8170 The Cybersecurity Framework
NISTIR 8176 Security Assurance Requirements for Linux Application Container Deployments
NISTIR 8179 Criticality Analysis Process Model
NISTIR 8183 Cybersecurity Framework Manufacturing Profile
NISTIR 8192 Enhancing Resilience of the Internet and Communications Ecosystem
Whitepaper Cybersecurity Framework Manufacturing Profile
Whitepaper NIST Framework for Improving Critical Infrastructure Cybersecurity
Whitepaper Challenging Security Requirements for US Government Cloud Computing Adoption
FIPS PUBS 140-2 Security Requirements for Cryptographic Modules
FIPS PUBS 140-2 Annex A Approved Security Functions
FIPS PUBS 140-2 Annex B Approved Protection Profiles
FIPS PUBS 140-2 Annex C Approved Random Number Generators
FIPS PUBS 140-2 Annex D Approved Key Establishment Techniques
FIPS PUBS 180-4 Secure Hash Standard (SHS)
FIPS PUBS 186-4 Digital Signature Standard (DSS)
FIPS PUBS 197 Advanced Encryption Standard (AES)
FIPS PUBS 198-1 The Keyed-Hash Message Authentication Code (HMAC)
FIPS PUBS 199 Standards for Security Categorization of Federal Information and Information Systems
FIPS PUBS 200 Minimum Security Requirements for Federal Information and Information Systems

CyberSecurity Standards Library™

FIPS PUBS 201-2	Personal Identity Verification (PIV) of Federal Employees and Contractors
FIPS PUBS 202	SHA-3 Standard: Permutation-Based Hash and Extendable-Output Functions

DHS Study DHS Study on Mobile Device Security

OMB A-130 / FISMA OMB A-130/Federal Information Security Modernization Act

DoD

UFC 3-430-11	Boiler Control Systems
UFC 4-010-06	Cybersecurity of Facility-Related Control Systems
FC 4-141-05N	Navy and Marine Corps Industrial Control Systems Monitoring Stations
MIL-HDBK-232A	RED/BLACK Engineering-Installation Guidelines
MIL-HDBK 1195	Radio Frequency Shielded Enclosures
TM 5-601	Supervisory Control and Data Acquisition (SCADA) Systems for C4ISR Facilities
ESTCP	Facility-Related Control Systems Cybersecurity Guideline
ESTCP	Facility-Related Control Systems Ver 4.0
DoD	Self-Assessing Security Vulnerabilities & Risks of Industrial Controls
DoD	Program Manager's Guidebook for Integrating the Cybersecurity Risk Management Framework (RMF) into the System Acquisition Lifecycle
DoD	Advanced Cyber Industrial Control System Tactics, Techniques, and Procedures (ACI TTP)

NERC

NERC CIP 002-5.1	Cyber Security — BES Cyber System Categorization
NERC CIP 003-6	Cyber Security — Security Management Controls
NERC CIP 003-7(i)	Cyber Security — Security Management Controls
NERC CIP 004-6	Cyber Security — Personnel & Training
NERC CIP 005-5	Cyber Security — Electronic Security Perimeter(s)
NERC CIP 006-6	Cyber Security — Physical Security of BES Cyber Systems
NERC CIP 007-6	Cyber Security — Systems Security Management
NERC CIP 008-5	Cyber Security — Incident Reporting and Response Planning
NERC CIP 009-6	Cyber Security — Recovery Plans for BES Cyber Systems
NERC CIP 010-2	Cyber Security — Configuration Change Management and Vulnerability
NERC CIP 011-2	Cyber Security — Information Protection
NERC CIP 014-2	Physical Security

Click on a title to obtain a printed copy of these standards at Amazon.com

www.ingramcontent.com/pod-product-compliance
Lightning Source LLC
Chambersburg PA
CBHW050937060326
40689CB00040B/621
* 9 7 8 1 9 7 8 2 1 8 4 7 5 *